Robert E. Park

THE CROWD AND THE PUBLIC

AND OTHER ESSAYS

Masse und Publikum is here translated into English for the first time.

THE UNIVERSITY OF CHICAGO PRESS, CHICAGO 60637
THE UNIVERSITY OF CHICAGO PRESS, LTD., LONDON

Printed in the United States of America

International Standard Book Number: 0–226–64609–2 (clothbound)
Library of Congress Catalog Card Number: 78–189361

Contents

Introduction

ROBERT E. PARK'S doctoral dissertation, *Masse und Publikum* (*The Crowd and the Public*), was published in 1904.[1] A perfect copy, recently encountered in a large university library, was yellowed and brittle but apparently undisturbed by any reader for sixty-five years. This may be symbolic of the attention paid, explicitly at least, by American sociology to the earliest work of one of its most influential pioneers. Seldom cited, the dissertation is sometimes even omitted from Park bibliographies. But as Everett C. Hughes has remarked, "The results of Park's work in those four years of study in Germany are diffused throughout American and even world sociology, even unto today."[2] To read *The Crowd and the Public* today is to experience the excitement of uncovering a seminal work—of discovering links between several intellectual traditions, both European and American; of seeing the initial formulation of concepts and interests found in later writing; and of sharing in the labors of a mind at work during the initial stages of a developing field. In addition, there are glimpses of figures who have long since dropped from view, such as Pasquale Rossi.[3]

1 Bern: Lack and Grunau.

2 Personal communication, November 2, 1970.

3 Rossi is an example of forgotten writers who may deserve to be rediscovered. Barnes and Becker assert that Rossi "brought out the best treatise on the psycho-sociology of the crowd and related social structures yet to appear in any language, *Sociologica e psicologia collettiva* (1904). It contains an excellent history of the theories of the field, and Rossi's own analysis gives evidence of great acumen." See Harry Elmer Barnes and

As a synthesizing effort, *The Crowd and the Public* cites and explicates the ideas of many, but it is perhaps the influence of Simmel and Le Bon which, in different ways, appears to be most dominant. On the conceptual and substantive levels, many of Park's later concerns emerge in this first work: competition, self-awareness, reciprocal interaction, process and change, characteristics of the sect, significance of strikes, focusing of social attention, social epidemics, and many more.

As Park relates it, he was led to the writing of *The Crowd and the Public* by a chain of circumstances beginning with his work as a newspaperman after college graduation. "The newspaper and news became my problem"—a problem that led him back to school at Harvard to study philosophy and then to Europe in search of "a fundamental point of view from which I could describe the behavior of society, under the influence of news, in the precise and universal language of science." While in Berlin for Simmel's lectures, Park encountered a treatise by Kistiakowski which seemed the first direct approach to the problem interesting him. Since Kistiaskowski had studied under Wilhelm Windelband, Park sought out Windelband and wrote *Masse und Publikum* under his direction.[4]

In its totality, *The Crowd and the Public* might be considered most relevant for two areas of sociology: collective behavior and basic theory, that is, the nature of sociology and the social bond.

Quite beyond the particular elements named in the title, there can already be seen developing in Park's first work a conception of sociology and its units of analysis. As with the specific topics of crowd and public, Park's later conception of the field is well under way. By analogy with the physical sciences, he seeks to identify the smallest meaningful particle for social analysis. Because of the role phenomenon, this particle cannot be the individual—in an important sense the individual is not the same in all

---

Howard Becker, *Social Thought from Lore to Science*, 2d ed. (Washington: Harren Press, 1952), 2:1008.

4 "An Autobiographical Note," in *The Collected Papers of Robert Ezra Park*, Vol. 1, *Race and Culture, 1913–1944* (Glencoe, Ill.: Free Press, 1950), pp. v–vi.

his group memberships. Thus, the basic units must be the types of relationships existing between individuals. The perspective is strongly reminiscent of Simmel, with whom Park had studied, and would today be seen as social-psychological.[5] Although subordinate to the conceptualizing of crowd, public, and other groups, an inquiry into the nature of social bonds runs throughout *The Crowd and the Public.* Each of the three chapters can be seen as analyzing a type of social unity: one derived from similarities; one from differences; and one from common norms, traditions, and culture. Unity based on similarities and differences immediately brings Durkheim to mind, but the use of the two principles of unity is very different for each writer. They are culturally structured for Durkheim, but seen as emergent interaction by Park.[6] These two elements of social unity are referred to again in the famous Park and Burgess *Introduction to the Science of Sociology.*[7]

Of interest is the question why the third theme, that of the General Will, was introduced. On one level, it emphasizes the traditional, stable, and normative element in all the other groups to which crowd and public are conceptually opposed. On another level, its use seems implicitly to admit the weakness of a strictly interactionist approach to social life. There is something in operation here which is more than simply the crystallization of past interactions. An example is Park's idea that public opinion, the product of the public, cannot create the fundamental norms under which the public operates. These norms are socially prior, existing at another level of reality. Nor do similarities in individual values

5 Ralph H. Turner, ed., *Robert E. Park on Social Control and Collective Behavior* (Chicago: University of Chicago Press, 1967), pp. xiv–xv.

6 One can only speculate as to whether Park had read *The Division of Labor* before writing *The Crowd and the Public;* there are footnote references to several items by Durkheim, but not to the *Division of Labor.* On the basis of extensive personal as well as formal academic contact with Park, the author of a recent survey of sociology argues that Park's "knowledge of Durkheim—and Weber for that matter—was slight or indifferent." See Edward Shils, "Tradition, Ecology, and Institution in the History of Sociology," *Daedalus* 99 (Fall 1970) : 789, also n. 27.

7 See Turner's discussion in *Park on Social Control,* Introduction.

imply common norms; the norm must be acceptable by all as applicable to all—Park's derivation from Rousseau is reminiscent of Angell's distinction between "common" and "like" values, a recent expression of a theme of long standing in social analysis.[8] From another viewpoint, the General Will chapter introduces a more strictly sociological perspective, which is all the more interesting because it is laboriously derived from nonsociological sources, in contrast to the essentially social-psychological framework of the first two chapters. Park's subsequent evaluation of cultural and interactionist approaches has been ably summarized elsewhere.[9] *The Crowd and the Public* demonstrates an early recognition of the deficiencies of each perspective used alone.

Park and Collective Behavior

"Crowd" and "public" will be recognized immediately as two of the traditional units treated by collective behavior, a field which Park himself named and launched as a distinct specialty within American sociology. *The Crowd and the Public* was not intended to do this, however, but to investigate the properties of two kinds of collectivities. Nevertheless the common features which distinguish them from other kinds of groups provide an implicit definition of the area encompassing both, for crowd and public represent "the processes through which new groups are formed" serving "to bring individuals out of old ties and into new ones."[10] Crowd and public do not have traditions and customs, but lead to their generation. Indeed, this all seems less ambiguous than the initial definition in the well-known chapter 13 of the *Introduction to the Science of Sociology*: "Collective behavior, then, is the behavior of individuals under the influence of an impulse that is common and collective, an impulse, in other words, that is the result of social interaction."[11] Here, all social behavior would seem to be "collective behavior."

8 Robert C. Angell, *Free Society and Moral Crisis* (Ann Arbor: University of Michigan Press, 1958), chap. 2 and notes.

9 Turner, Introduction to *Park on Social Control.*

10 *The Crowd and the Public*, p. 78.

11 Robert E. Park and Ernest W. Burgess, *Introduction to the Science of Sociology* (Chicago: University of Chicago Press, 1921), p. 865.

The thrust of *The Crowd and the Public* clearly anticipates the actual use of the collective behavior concept in the *Introduction*, including a redefinition later in chapter 13 where it is described as "the processes by which societies are disintegrated into their constituent elements and the processes by which these elements are brought together again into new relations to form new organizations and new societies."[12] The idea of collective behavior resulting in social and cultural change has remained central to the concept through the present.

The other fundamental elements or connotations of collective behavior may also be derived from Park's earlier ideas. Spontaneous, short-lived, ephemeral are adjectives often applied to collective behavior groupings. Park saw crowd and public as groups without a past or a future; once formed, they either disperse or are transformed into stable groups subject to a normative order. And if such groups are seen as "without tradition" and as acting to change the institutional order, it may be possible to deduce them as existing apart from, outside of, or in "gaps" in that order. Today, tentative agreement on what constitutes collective behavior would focus on the idea of extra-institutional behavior. Some kinds of this behavior, panic, for example—do not necessarily lead to changes in the institutional order.

Park's emphasis in *The Crowd and the Public* on the concept of the General Will heightens the contrast between the stable normative order and collective behavior existing apart from it. In his later work, Park used Sumner's conception of the mores to represent the stability to which collective behavior is conceptually and empirically opposed. Written before *Folkways* appeared, *The Crowd and the Public* ingeniously uses concepts from political philosophy to emphasize supra-individual tradition, custom, and norm.

Crowd and public, then, are for Park the two basic categories of change-inducing, extra-institutional behavior. That they remained central to his thinking is reflected in their prominence in chapters 12 and 13 of the *Introduction* and in his "Collective Behavior" entry in the 1935 *Encyclopedia of the Social Sciences*. Park also frequently taught a course under the title "Crowd and

12 Ibid., p. 924–25.

Public."[13] Other kinds of collective behavior—the sect, the mass movement, revolution—are mentioned in passing in *The Crowd and the Public.* Park's later development of these other forms can be seen fundamentally as extensions of the two basic concepts. "The sect, religious or political, may be regarded as a perpetuation and permanent form of the orgiastic (ecstatic) or expressive crowd."[14] "All great mass movements tend to display, to a greater or less extent, the characteristics that Le Bon attributes to crowds."[15] "A revolution is a mass movement which seeks to change the mores by destroying the existing social order."[16] Social movements share the characteristics of both the crowd and the public. In addition to the above quote citing Le Bon, Park wrote, "When these changes [in public opinion] take a definite direction and have or seem to have a definite goal, we call the phenomenon a social movement."[17]

After a theory of collective behavior has defined its units, some explanation of their behavior is called for. Explanations may be categorized as emphasizing internal or external factors. For example, is a riot explained by looking at processes of interaction, communication, leadership, etc., within the acting collectivity, or should the focus rest on the discontents, political structure, etc., objective or perceived, in the social setting?

Following Simmel's overall emphasis on types of interpersonal interaction and Le Bon's specific assertions about crowd dynamics, Park in *The Crowd and the Public* clearly concentrates on "internal" factors. Certainly the setting is not ignored: "Precisely because the crowd proves to be a social power whose effect is always more or less disruptive and revolutionary, it seldom arises where there is social stability and where customs have deep roots. In contrast, where social bonds are removed and old institutions

13 Robert E. L. Faris, *Chicago Sociology: 1920–1932* (San Francisco: Chandler, 1967), p. 106.

14 Park and Burgess, *Introduction,* p. 872.

15 Ibid., p. 871.

16 Ibid., p. 934.

17 Park and Burgess, *Introduction,* chap. 12, reprinted in Turner, *Park on Social Control,* p. 216.

weakened, great crowd movements develop more easily and forcefully."[18] Crowd and public appear "wherever a new interest asserts itself"; conflict of interests produces a public.[19] Like Le Bon in *The Crowd*, however, Park does not expand these remarks on the setting, and they are not an integrated or major part of the analysis. Later, in the *Introduction*, "social unrest" does of course become a key concept, although it is presented ambiguously as both a characteristic of the setting and a form of collective behavior.[20] In *The Crowd and the Public* the two kinds of collectivities are differentiated entirely in terms of internal dynamics; individual psychological differences alone lead to participation in crowd or public.[21] There is no explicit statement as to what, if anything, in the social setting would tend to produce one or the other kind of collectivity. A clue may be offered however, by the argument in chapter 3 that a minimal normative framework must be present if the public is to operate. Is Park suggesting that normative ambiguity, inadequacy, and breakdown extending beyond a certain point will produce a crowd rather than a public?

Park's specific explanatory mechanisms for the characteristics of crowd behavior seem to derive from two sources: (1) the similar assertions of Sighele and Le Bon with regard to suggestibility, unanimity, intolerance, emotionality, etc., and (2) a synthesis of various psychological approaches seen by Park as dealing with kinds of imitation. Clearly present in the second category are ideas of crowd milling and circular reaction which subsequently were given increasing prominence in the *Introduction* and in Herbert Blumer's landmark discussion of this whole approach in the *Outline of the Principles of Sociology*, a book initially edited by Park himself.[22]

Park's description of the public in *The Crowd and the Public* is more difficult to follow, but like his discussion of the crowd, it includes all the basic elements of "public" later to appear in the

18 *The Crowd and the Public*, p. 47.
19 Ibid., p. 79.
20 Park and Burgess, *Introduction*, p. 866.
21 *The Crowd and the Public*, p. 80.
22 New York: Barnes & Noble, 1939.

Introduction: reasoned discussion of issues, based on opposed interests, but carried out within a framework understood by all—a "universe of discourse," to use Park's later phrase.[23]

In *The Crowd and the Public*, the fundamental distinctions between the two types are simply stated: the crowd suppresses the differences among its members and uncritically, emotionally, unanimously fixes its attention upon some object; the public is the polar opposite in its recognition of individual differences in value and interest, in its engaging in rational discussion and debate, and in arriving at a consensus which does not impose unanimity on its members. Suggestibility is "precisely the characteristic trait of the crowd"; it results in the crowd finally becoming "the plastic instrument of its leader, whose suggestion is followed without any resistance."[24] Park implies that this does not happen in the more critical and rational public, although he does mention the manipulation of what is commonly called "public opinion."[25]

Park's distinction between crowd and public directly raises another important continuing issue in collective behavior theory: rationality, or the lack of it. Without here defining rational or irrational, the characteristics imputed to crowd behavior by Sighele and Le Bon would usually be seen as irrational: suggestibility, emotionality, intolerance, rapid reversals of attention, lack of critical ability, expression of base instincts, etc. Furthermore, within the Western intellectual tradition such attributes are negatively judged. Looking at popular riots and revolutionary movements, the early European writers did not like what they saw and condemned such outbursts for the irrational features perceived in them. While Park is explicitly aware of the danger of political bias in these interpretations, he seems to accept Le Bon's analysis as a "scientific" attempt and does not alter it in any significant way. Generally uncritical references to Le Bon, except for objection to the lack of precision, continue in the *Introduction*; and Blumer's

23 Park and Burgess, *Introduction*, chap. 12, as reprinted in Turner, *Park on Social Control*, p. 216.
24 *The Crowd and the Public*, p. 47.
25 Ibid., p. 57.

account[26] heightens, if anything, the portrayal of the maddened and irrational mob. In *The Crowd and the Public* Park is careful to state that his analysis of the difference between the two kinds of collectivity does not imply a judgment,[27] but this can only be taken as a formal disclaimer.

Despite his acceptance of the Le Bon–Sighele portrayal of crowd behavior, however, Park's inclusion of the public within the category of change-inducing groups radically altered the thrust of their tradition, for an irrational mechanism of change is now balanced by a mechanism that is rational and reasonable, even if the conditions giving rise to one or the other are not made clear. As already remarked, Park incorporates elements of both the crowd and the public in his later discussion of social movements, and if a reading-between-the-lines guess may be ventured, there is somewhat more emphasis on the relative rationality of movements.

Finally, any perspective on collective behavior must handle the problem of relating such behavioral mechanisms to everyday, institutionalized behavior. This poses no logical difficulties for Park in *The Crowd and the Public*—the whole point of the central section is to relate concepts from contemporary individual psychology, emerging social psychology, imitation theory, and the interactionist orientation of Simmel so that crowd, public, and all other forms of social behavior can be explained in the same terms. While much of the specific material is now dated, there remains a theoretical unity often lacking in subsequent collective behavior theory.

In *The Crowd and the Public*, then, Park dealt with four fundamental, continuing issues in collective behavior: (1) conception and definition of the field and its units; (2) specific explanations of those units, explanations tending to stress either factors internal to the units, or external to them, in the social setting; (3) the rationality issue; and (4) the relationship between collective behavior and other kinds of social behavior.

26 Alfred M. Lee, ed., *New Outline of the Principles of Sociology* (New York: Barnes & Noble, 1951), pp. 180–81.
27 *The Crowd and the Public*, p. 81.

Collective Behavior Theory After Park

Recent work in collective behavior, in dealing with the issues discussed above, has departed from Park's founding contributions, but it has also returned to them, sometimes in surprising ways. For perhaps thirty years, Park's conception of the field, its units, and its explanatory principles held unchallenged dominance among sociologists. These principles are still those most frequently relied upon both in general introductory course treatments and in texts for the field of collective behavior itself. The 1957 Turner and Killian *Collective Behavior* acknowledged that "the ideas in the book reflect most directly the tradition established by Robert E. Park and Ernest W. Burgess, and subsequently extended by Herbert Blumer."[28] Although Kurt and Gladys Engel Langs's *Collective Dynamics* (1961) discusses various traditions of analysis, it seems essentially to represent a combination of Le Bon via Park with a Freudian orientation.[29] The first radical attempt to reorient collective behavior theory became apparent with the appearance of Smelser's book in 1963,[30] which according to one opinion "should prove to be the contribution most relevant to research in the seventies."[31] Turner has recently directed important criticisms at traditional approaches, particularly those derived from Le Bon and Freud; he has tried to bring together the explanations of collective behavior and those used elsewhere in sociology, as well as to account more realistically for observed crowd behavior.[32] Somewhat earlier, collective behavior was viewed by Swanson as activity directed toward problem-solving. Although he wrote from within the Park tradition, Swanson al-

28 Ralph H. Turner and Lewis M. Killian, *Collective Behavior* (Englewood Cliffs, N.J.: Prentice-Hall, 1957), p. vi.

29 New York: Thomas Y. Crowell.

30 Neil J. Smelser, *Theory of Collective Behavior* (New York: Free Press of Glencoe, 1963).

31 Robert R. Evans, ed., *Readings in Collective Behavior* (Chicago: Rand McNally, 1969), p. 13.

32 Ralph H. Turner, "Collective Behavior," in Robert E. L. Faris, ed., *Handbook of Modern Sociology* (Chicago: Rand McNally, 1964).

tered the focus of concern by stressing that differing group perceptions of the problem situation led to different kinds of collective behavior.[33]

Conception of the Field and Its Units

Among the challenges to the Park tradition posed by these varied approaches, there is little agreement in regard to the focal issues previously suggested. Perhaps all theorists would agree on some scale of complexity and stability in collective behavior, with crowds, panics, and fads at one end and organized social movements at the other. Some theorists indeed argue that social movements are too patterned and enduring to be included within the general topic.[34] Turner suggests instead of a typology, a continuum of increasingly complex responses to increasingly severe breakdowns or inadequacies in the normative order.[35] Smelser's units include panic, craze, hostile outburst, norm- and value-oriented movements. Perhaps one source of enduring confusion is the fact that some of the units suggested appear to be behavioral processes (e.g., panic), while others (e.g., the crowd) are collectivities. If some commonly treated units are sorted out according to these categories, a tentative agreement might be established as follows:

PROCESSES	Panic	Craze or Fad	Hostile Outburst or Riot	Intended Social Change (Reform–Revolution)
COLLECTIVITIES	Mass/Crowd	Mass	Crowd	Social Movement

The concept of the public is missing from this array. Such an exclusion can be justified on two grounds. By the accident of

33 G. E. Swanson, "A Preliminary Laboratory Study of the Acting Crowd," *American Sociological Review* 18 (October 1953): 522–33; idem, "Social Change in the Urban Society," in Ronald Freedman et al., *Principles of Sociology*, 1st ed., (New York: Henry Holt, 1952), chap. 14.

34 Evans, *Readings*, p. viii; Roger Brown, *Social Psychology* (New York: Free Press of Glencoe, 1965), p. 728.

35 Turner, "Collective Behavior," p. 394.

scholarly jurisdiction, the study of public opinion and communication has become since Park's day a separate field with its own body of concepts, theory, and research. More important, if collective behavior refers to extra-institutional behavior, the public-opinion process would not be included, since in democratic, and perhaps in all modern societies, it is a vital part of the institutional order.

Explanatory Orientations

The most dramatic changes to occur since Park's work have been concerned with explanations of collective behavior, both in regard to the external-internal focus and to explanatory mechanisms. A general tendency has been to increase attention paid to the settings producing collective behavior, and to try to differentiate their features. Thus Swanson argued that differential perceptions, along several dimensions, of problems in the social environment would produce the different responses of panic, dynamic crowd, social movement, public, and mass behavior.[36] Smelser has a standard set of six "determinants" operative in producing any kind of collective behavior.[37] Four of these determinants refer to the setting: structural conduciveness, structural strain, precipitating factors, and social control. (These are formal categories whose contents differ for various kinds of collective behavior.) In Turner's current formulation, the significant feature of the setting appears to be increasing severity of normative inadequacy ranging from situations in which norms are lacking or ambiguous through those in which prior organization is disrupted to those where satisfaction of needs dictates that the normative order be set aside.[38]

Park's emphasis was on the internal mechanisms active in both crowd and public; this approach, ultimately deriving from Le Bon, long remained dominant. Smelser has been the most vocal revisionist here. Two of his six determinants, the spread of a gen-

36 Swanson, "Social Change in the Urban Society," p. 564.
37 Smelser, *Theory*, pp. 15–17.
38 Turner, "Collective Behavior," pp. 394–97.

eralized belief and mobilization for action, call attention to internal processes, but Smelser insists that, for the theory, it is not important what kind of internal processes fulfill these conditions.[39] It is only necessary that some sort of interaction, communication, and leadership appear. Turner's "emergent norm" label for his approach directs attention to an internal process: inherent in any instance of collective behavior are formation of a new collective definition of the situation, development of new norms appropriate to it, legitimation or justification of these norms, and attempts to enforce conformity.[40] This approach is congruent to Swanson's earlier and less fully developed ideas; it also awakens interesting echoes of Park. Although part of Turner's theory is a rejection of the Le Bon–derived explanation of crowd which Turner finds both theoretically and empirically untenable,[41] his emergent norm process in its most general terms might be seen as roughly parallel to Park's concept of the public with its lack of unanimity, more rational approach, and development of new norms.

The Rationality Issue

Explicitly at least, the most important change in recent years on the issue of rationality has been rejection of the European insistence on viewing collective behavior as intrinsically irrational. Recognition of political and social bias in this viewpoint, more exact observation of episodes of behavior, and the lingering but final demise of the "suggestion" doctrine at the hands of psychologists all played their part.[42] Few theorists today would attempt simply to reverse the long-standing bias and posit a rational collective behavior acting against the irrational institutional order, but modern emphasis on such processes as attempted problem-

39 Smelser, *Theory*, pp. 10–11.

40 Turner, "Collective Behavior," p. 397.

41 Ibid., pp. 384–92.

42 On bias see Leon Bramson, *The Political Context of Sociology* (Princeton: Princeton University Press, 1961), chap. 3; on observation see Turner, "Collective Behavior," p. 390; on the suggestion doctrine see Solomon E. Asch, *Social Psychology* (New York: Prentice-Hall, 1952), chap. 14.

solving and definition of an ambiguous situation are examples of how far explanations have tended to move away from the earlier stress on emotional contagion and suppression of all critical abilities.

A curious treatment of rationality appears in Smelser's argument, however. Creation of a "generalized belief" which provides a basis for action is one of his determinants of collective behavior; application of the generalized belief to a real situation always involves a process called "short-circuiting."[43] Smelser denies seeing collective behavior as essentially irrational,[44] but his "generalized belief" could more aptly be labelled "overgeneralized," as it by definition contains conclusions more general than the evidence supports. Similarly, "short-circuiting" means that a conceptual jump from general notions to concrete action always bypasses levels of qualification, hence leading to unrealistic thought and action.[45] Thus, emphasis on irrationality has reappeared by an entirely new route. And if Turner's emphasis echoes Park's idea of the public, this portion of Smelser's approach seems to recall the crowd with its irrational unanimity.

Collective Behavior and Institutionalized Behavior

Finally, both Smelser and Turner attempt to use principles explaining collective behavior which are no different from those applicable to institutionalized behavior. Smelser's theory is based on a general scheme of categories capable of classifying all social behavior; collective behavior types are differentiated according to which of the various universal "components of action" they attempt to change or restructure.[46] Part of Turner's critique of the continuing influence of the "contagion" tradition, within which Park is found, is the tradition's assumption that "crowds require a level of psychological explanation which organized groups do

43 Smelser, *Theory*, p. 72.
44 Ibid., p. 11.
45 Ibid., pp. 72–73.
46 Ibid., chap. 5.

not require."[47] For Turner the normative process is central in sociology; it applies to collective behavior as well as elsewhere.

In summary then, a survey of the present state of collective behavior theory suggests that departures from Park's approach have not as yet resulted in any new consensus about some of the most basic concerns of the field. There does appear to be tentative agreement on devoting increased attention to the social setting, dropping dated social-psychological concepts, and decreasing the emphasis on supposed irrational characteristics.

The Crowd as a Relevant Contemporary Concept

What has been gained and lost since Park's work appeared? What in it may be considered still valid or suggestive today?

A clue from one recent study suggests that models derived from different theoretical perspectives may be approximated at different stages of a collective episode. In attempting to account for the spread of a hysterical belief, investigators found that a "social isolate" theory based upon ideas of isolation and deviance, a "group influence" theory utilizing sociometric channels, and a "contagion" theory from classic collective behavior all seemed to fit successively as the episode developed.[48] This suggests that some of the traditional concepts may still be useful, not as total explanations, but when restricted to specific conditions.

If the crowd is taken as a valid unit of analysis, current reorientations in theory appear to have done little to advance understanding of what actually takes place among its members. Criticizing a trend in current theory, Herbert Blumer insists that complete analysis of a crowd situation demands more than merely identifying "(a) the social conditions out of which crowds emerge, (b) the forms of overt behavior in which they engage, and (c) the social consequences of such overt behavior." Such an approach misses the significant "analytic consideration of collective excite-

47 Turner, "Collective Behavior," p. 386.

48 Alan C. Kerckhoff and Kurt W. Back, *The June Bug* (New York: Appleton-Century Crofts, 1968), chap. 6.

ment (the basic condition in crowd behavior)."[49] Much of the flavor of crowd action does seem to have vanished in the most recent theoretical approaches. Perhaps there has been an over-compensation for the excesses of Le Bon.

Finally, even if Park's analysis of crowd and public no longer appears adequate, his emphasis on the rational and the irrational, unanimous and nonunanimous alternatives in change is still a valid point of reference. His focus on these alternatives is as pertinent to the problems of evaluating calls to political commitment as it is to the current renewal of interest in the modes and mechanisms of social change.

The Continuity in Park's Work

Three essays written by Park much later in his life—"Social Planning and Human Nature" (1935), "Reflections on Communication and Culture" (1938), and "Symbiosis and Socialization" (1939)—are included in this volume to illustrate the continuity and development of themes first appearing in *The Crowd and the Public.*

"Social Planning and Human Nature" emphasizes the interplay and balance of the rational and nonrational; the traditional and static tendency in human life is juxtaposed with the shared problems, unrest, social movements, and political processes bringing about change. Park argues that the strength of cultural tradition and the nonrational, unpredictable qualities of human nature are formidable barriers to rationally planned change. On the other hand, the "Utopian" plan, whose rationality is so aggressively explicit that it usually appears irrational, can have paradoxical latent consequences. It may serve as a reference point for social criticism, thus aiding in the formation of public opinion and political power, or it may become a new myth giving cohesion to a social movement. Here the boundaries of the religious movement appear to fade into those of the secular political movement.

49 Herbert Blumer, "The Justice of the Crowd," review of George Rudé, *The Crowd in History*, in *Trans-Action* 2 (September–October 1965): 43.

As the rational and nonrational are inextricably bound together, so are cultural constraint and social change. If plans for change are to be workable, they must be consistent with "local tradition and customary order." And yet the modern political process itself is precisely the deliberate disturbance of that customary social order. The new political products must ultimately be "assimilated, digested, and incorporated with the folkways of the original and historic society." Following Hume's usage, Park sees government resting upon opinion, opinion here including the mores and the culture as well as current responses to events and doctrines.

The other two essays written in 1938 and 1939 clearly show how Park's lifelong interest in communication and collective behavior was related to those other topics for which he is well known: the ecological, social, and moral orders; competition, conflict, and cultural assimilation; and community and urban life. In "Reflections on Communication and Culture," Park states that communication is a fundamental process in human affairs because meaning or interpretation is crucial to distinctly human interaction. Meaning is shared through the mechanism of culture which includes "all that is communicable."

The two basic forms of communication are pointed out again, the first more rational and the second more emotional; one communicating ideas, the other expressing feeling. The first form is exemplified in news; the other in art, literature, and currently, motion pictures. In general, the communication process promotes group stability by providing common understandings, regulating competition, coordinating the division of labor, and assuring intergenerational continuity.

The communication process also contributes to change. Unrest leading to collective behavior may be communicated either more rationally or more expressively. News provides a basis for action, while expressive communication increases understanding of different cultures, hence acculturation. If competition differentiates individuals and groups, communication integrates. By expanding shared understandings, this integration or acculturation causes change. Focal points in the communication process are the great cities: "If the market place is the center from which news is disseminated and cultural influences are diffused, it is, likewise, the center in which old ideas go into the crucible and new ideas emerge." In the modern world, groups previously in isolation are brought into self-conscious conflict, and the definitions which must result from this conflict lay the basis for further communication and acculturation.

"Symbiosis and Socialization" is a remarkable essay, containing in a few pages a lifework's reflections on the varied dimensions of social life. References range from Le Bon and Mannheim to G. H. Mead and the plant and animal ecologists. Park sees man as part of the web of life, sharing some characteristics with both plant and animal communities. But each of these forms of life has its unique elements. Only in plant communities does complete competition reign. Animal communities are social and sometimes elaborately organized; this would suggest that there exists a form of communication among members. The apparent similarities to human communication and human social behavior are, however, deceptive. At this point Park returns to Le Bon's simplest model of collective behavior, milling and interstimulation. Park now tests this model as an example of uniquely human behavior. The milling herd can never attain a focused, deliberate collective act. Instead, characteristically human collective behavior is that which is based on meaningful communication and results in the formation of institutions. These institutions in turn regulate and modify the basic ecological processes in which man participates together with other life.

The pages in this essay devoted to collective behavior both restate and refine Park's fundamental contributions to the field. In contrast to collective behavior based on meaningful communication, expressive collective behavior is seen as similar to animal milling: it does not result in concerted action directed toward a goal. Indeed, the communication which creates a consensus on group goals is really what underlay that vague phrase used by many writers, "the collective mind." The processes for reaching such goals are the crowd and the public, expressions of unanimity and diversity. From Karl Mannheim's *Ideology and Utopia*, Park draws the idea that society needs and creates its directing doctrines. He believed that the creation of such doctrines corresponded more closely with his concept of the public than with that of the crowd. Publics with their ideologies are characteristic of the modern political society and its rationality, rather than of traditional and familial organization.

Collective action under emergency conditions is also the origin of many social institutions developed out of the more organized form of collective behavior—social movements. "Not every social movement terminates in a new institution, but the necessity of carrying on programs initiated in some social emergency has been responsible for many if not most modern and recent institutions."

For Park, the trend of history and social evolution is inevitably toward an increasingly diverse, yet increasingly interdependent ecological, political, and moral order:

> Thus the web of life which holds within its meshes all living organisms is visibly tightening, and there is in every part of the world obviously a growing interdependence of all living creatures; a vital interdependence that is more extensive and intimate today than at any other period in the course of the long historical process.

HENRY ELSNER, JR.

Note on The Crowd and the Public

Masse und Publikum is a gem of sustained thought and critical reflection. I believe it has been greatly underestimated, not least because of Park's own depreciation of the manuscript and the fact that it has never been available in English translation.

I

The general character of the work was inspired by Simmel's conception of sociology as the science of social forms. The expressed objective of *Masse und Publikum* is to determine the generic characteristics of "two basic forms of sociological entities" (*zwei Grundformen* [der] *soziologischen Einheiten*), the crowd* and the public. Methodologically, Park's aim is to achieve a maximum of clarity and precision in the construction of scientific concepts, a concern most immediately stimulated by Rickert. Substantively, the dissertation involves a synthesis of three traditions of social thought: group psychology, individual psychology, and political philosophy.

Each of the three chapters of the dissertation focuses on one of these three traditions. The first chapter, "Die Masse," begins with a critical review of the literature on crowd behavior as found in the works of Sighele, Le Bon, Tarde, Rossi, and Sidis. Park

*Park uses the term *Masse* throughout, although it is not always clear when he is referring to crowds and when to a diffuse mass as represented, for example, by all those affected by advertising.

then proceeds to reject as scientifically unviable two popular conceptions of the crowd: that it is equivalent to rioting behavior, and that it is to be viewed as a collection of spatially contiguous individuals. He notes that the principal proponents of group psychology rather define the crowd in terms of psychic interaction. This characterization is by itself not adequate, however. Park concludes by defining the crowd as a phenomenon involving reciprocal stimulation in which the whole interaction process is directed toward a single common goal.

II

Chapter 2, "Der soziologische Prozess," begins with a search for a theory that will combine the individualistic approach of political economy with the collectivistic approach of group psychology. The ingredients for such a "synthetic discipline" are to be found in imitation theory. The forerunners of the theory of imitation are Butler, Hume, and Adam Smith; its contemporary exponents are Tarde, Baldwin, and Giddings. The crucial sociological importance of the imitation process is that it serves to transmit culture, and to communicate constraints from the group as a whole to the individual. This primary interaction, spreading and generalizing ways of acting through imitation, is for Tarde the specifically "social."

Other kinds of processes are involved, however, when groups act to reshape their orientations—processes exhibited in the deliberations of parliaments or courts of justice. These processes appear in simplest form in the behavior of the crowd. Crowd behavior is characterized above all by a concentration of attention on a single object. The immediate consequence of this heightened collective attentiveness is an inhibition of customary impulses and associations that results in increased suggestibility. Through social attentiveness in the crowd, customs and stable forms of intercourse are loosened and finally dissolved. Mass movements thus have the dual role of destroying existing institutions and preparing the spirit of new ones.

Another basic form of interaction which serves to reorient

group attitudes is that of the public. In developing his conception of the public, Park draws on Tarde's concept of counter-imitation, Baldwin's and Royce's concept of opposition, and Simmel's ideas about social differentiation and exchange. Exchange is a "secondary" form of interaction. It also involves a kind of imitative responsiveness to others, in that one sets oneself so as to sympathize with the point of view of the other, but then one acts in a direction contrary to that of the other. It is this combination of entertaining the ideas and attitudes of others with assertion of personal interests that constitutes the essential structure of the public.

In the crowd, all purely personal impulses are suppressed. Only those ideas which fit in with the ideas sustained by the collective interaction process are active in the minds of individual participants. In the public, individual impulses and interests emerge against a background of common information and are developed further through the interaction process. Whereas crowd behavior remains at the level of common perception, public behavior, expressed through public opinion, results from discussion and deliberations based on a consideration of facts. In the crowd, existential and normative considerations are fused; all members have the same view of reality and what to do about it. In the public these dimensions are separated. The same perception of empirical realities is shared by all members of the public, but their value orientations regarding these things are diverse. Because of this, because the practical orientations of the public must refer to "theoretical" observations which provide materials for deliberation, the public is subordinated to theoretic norms. Independently established theoretical standards are the necessary precondition for the public. They introduce a new force into the collective life, a force that is not present in the crowd.

The public seeks to find its will through deliberation, to evaluate the diverse individual preferences from a supra-individual point of view. But it is characteristic of the public that it never definitively attains this standpoint. This is because it lacks consensus on practical norms. The public is not a norm-giving body. Norms and laws are grounded on established traditions, which are never equivalent to the vagaries of group life. They represent still another structural dimension, that represented by the concept of the general will.

III

Chapter 3, "Der Gesamtwille," discusses the evolution of the idea of the general will from Hobbes, Locke, and Rousseau through Kant, Fichte, and Hegel. The ethical substance which Hegel calls morality can be identified with Rousseau's concept of the *volonté générale*. This psychic substance is manifest subjectively in the individual mind as conscience and objectively in the form of the mores. The negative reactions of the totality aroused by the immoral behavior of an individual are an expression of this general will. This, not social interaction, is the source of obligatory norms: they represent a collective response for the protection of collective values.

Institutionalized social groups—castes, classes, sects, political parties, etc.—are therefore characterized by two distinct levels of psychological reality: (1) interaction—the action and adjustive reaction of human drives on one another, and (2) a general will manifest as a collective drive that subsumes all individual wills, and that even at times may stand opposed to the momentary impulses of the totality of individuals.

The crowd and the public stand in contrast to all such established groups. They are types of association which bring individuals out of their existing bonds and into new ones. Structurally more primitive than established groups, they exist empirically afterward. They differ from the other types of groups, not with respect to the content of their collective consciences, but their form. The crowd and the public are governed by a collective drive, but one that has not yet crystallized into a norm. They do not possess a general will in the traditional sense of the term, but represent an empirical forestage thereto. Neither crowds nor publics possess rules, modes of conscious governance, self-consciousness, or boundary maintenance. They are limited only by the immanent conditions of spontaneous interaction.

While crowds and publics are similar as fluid social forms

which serve to mediate social change, they differ in that the public is critical whereas the crowd is mindless. One needs only the capacity to feel and empathize to be a member of a crowd. To belong to a public, one must not only feel but be able to think and to understand the thoughts of others. Though not subject to practical regulations, one must adhere to the norms of logic.

Crowd and public are the only truly individualistic social forms. In the crowd we find anarchy in its purest form. In a public the individual stands only under the norms of logic, though the ultimate tyranny, as Max Stirner observed, is the tyranny of concepts.

IV

Park's dissertation is notable in several respects. It is probably the first attempt to formulate a functional interpretation of crowd behavior. Previously such phenomena had been viewed merely as threats to civil order and high culture or, at best, as involving deteriorated states of human functioning. *Masse und Publikum* shows the necessity for society to have such fluid, primitive forms to enable it to make institutional change.

Park's conceptualization of the distinction between crowd and public is a brilliant feat of intellectual differentiation. It has largely been lost sight of in later discussions of mass society and public opinion. It provides eloquent grounds for arguing the importance of professional journalism in democratic society, an implication not drawn out in the dissertation but well understood in Park's own life.

Masse und Publikum presents the first synthesis of two conceptions of the "social" which have stimulated much of modern sociology: Durkheim's (and Sumner's) notion of the social as a body of normative constraints, and Simmel's conception of the social in terms of forms of interaction. While Simmel considered norms to be of secondary interest, and Durkheim's approach neglected the actual processes of interaction, Park achieved a bifocal awareness of these two dimensions of social organization.

Finally, it might be noted that the analytic scheme which

Park adumbrated in this dissertation shows a striking parallel to the famous typology of types of authority which Weber was to work out some years later. The stages of imitation of custom, concerted action based on emotion, and public deliberation leading to the promulgation of new norms by established bodies show an obvious correspondence to the Weberian categories of traditionality, charismatic authority, and rational-legal authority. What Park has done is to look at the social psychological underbelly of these types of authority—a type of analysis which social scientists are today coming to regard as deeply significant.

From the point of view of Park's intellectual biography, the dissertation is also of considerable interest. One finds him there laboriously working out many of the basic ideas which were to guide some of his most important contributions to sociology two decades later: the concept of concerted action; the distinction between two levels of group life, one governed by norms and one not; the role of impartially presented information in the life of publics; and the relationship between elementary collective behavior and social change.

DONALD N. LEVINE

I. The Crowd and the Public

Curriculum Vitae

I WAS born in Harveyville, Pennsylvania, and first attended school in Redwing, Minnesota. After graduating from high school there, I studied for a year at the University of Minnesota in Minneapolis, then four years at the University of Michigan in Ann Arbor. My areas of study were literature [*Philologie*] and history, and my special interest, philosophy, was pursued under John Dewey. In 1887 I received a bachelor of philosophy degree.

For the next twelve years I worked as a reporter and editor in Minneapolis, Detroit, Denver, New York, and Chicago. The one important position I held during this time was a city editorship in Detroit. I decided to return to the university, and after one year's study at Harvard, I received a master of arts degree. At Harvard I studied psychology under Hugo Münsterberg and philosophy under Josiah Royce and William James.

In fall 1899 I went to Germany and attended the lectures of Friedrich Paulsen and Georg Simmel in Berlin for one semester. In fall 1900 I enrolled at the University of Strassburg where I studied philosophy under Wilhelm Windelband and Theobald Ziegler. As cognates, I studied political economy under Georg Knapp and geography with Georg Gerland. In spring 1903 I followed Professor Windelband to his new appointment in Heidelberg, where in addition to philosophy I studied geography with Alfred Hettner and political economy under Karl Rathgen.

In accordance with dissertation form in German universities, Robert Park included a brief description of his life and studies (*Lebenslauf*).

For my initial interest in philosophy I am indebted to John Dewey; William James and Josiah Royce were also important. The approach presented in this study is that of Wilhelm Windelband and Hugo Münsterberg. The final development of my philosophical ideas owes most to the influence of Wilhelm Windelband.

1904 ROBERT E. PARK

1

THE CROWD

I

THE IDEA of the social group is one of the most useful concepts emerging from recent studies in psychology. Of all the different forms of groupings displayed by a highly complex social life, the crowd and its types is one which has attracted the close attention of sociologists. Out of this interest developed crowd or collective psychology, a field which sees the prototype of social groups in loosely bound or unorganized collectivities, such as political parties or any casual gathering of people.

Crowd psychology is thus a new arrival among the sciences. As a new science, if it can even be called one, it is still forced to work with vaguely defined concepts. Since there is no previous scientific tradition, the exact definitions needed for its objects are also nonexistent. The ability to differentiate, define, and identify the facts with which any science begins, presumes a more or less established terminology.

The weakness of the terminology expected to describe crowd phenomena with theoretical precision is revealed in such words as "crowd," "nationality," "sect," and others. Used in everyday speech to designate different kinds of groups, these words are permeated with varying degrees of value or political biases. They can never be freed from such biases, even though a purely theoretical use is attempted, as in the study of crowd psychology. Nor is this the only difficulty. These terms have varying meanings for different writers and sometimes even for the same writer, where a continuous vacillation in meaning can occur, depending on whether the author has one or another example in mind.[1]

This writer believes that every significant advance in sociology must, in the last analysis, proceed with research like that begun in the field of crowd psychology, that is, the description and explanation of the activities of human groups. Both an examination of material already available and a more exact definition of the relevant concepts appears not only highly desirable but essential. The following study proposes to do this in the case of two basic forms of social units: the crowd and the public.

II

The first attempt to define the essence of the crowd with scientific precision was apparently made by Scipio Sighele, an Italian criminologist. In 1891 his *La Folla delinquenta* was published, a book written completely in the spirit of the Italian school of positive criminal law, and intended as a contribution to the solution of the problem of collective and individual responsibility. Even earlier, the medically influenced juridical literature had presented a series of inquiries into the phenomenon of social epidemics, especially those epidemics of crime which frequently manifest themselves as unmistakable crowd lawlessness. Tarde, for example, in *La Philosophie pénale* clearly points to the crowd as a distinct social phenomenon deserving of scientific study.[2]

The significance of Sighele's work lay in its attempt to combine all these manifestations of social epidemics into one concept. Sighele viewed the crowd phenomenon through the special viewpoint of his school, and thus he tended to consider it rare and abnormal that individuals who normally do not rebel against the

1 Compare the use of the word "crowd" in Sighele's early book, *La Coppia criminale,* with its use in the later work of the same author, *La Delinquenza settaria.* In the first work, the crowd is identified with the rabble; in the second, in contrast, under crowd is understood a nucleus of social organization out of which all other forms can eventually develop. See Kurella's German translation of Sighele's first-mentioned work, *Psychologie des Auflaufs und der Massenverbrechen,* pp. 40ff., and for the second, a French translation, *Psychologie des sectes,* p. 46.

2 Tarde, *La Philosophie pénale,* p. 320.

restrictions of custom and law lose their usual moral stability and self-control under the influence of crowd excitement and behave not like humans, but like raging animals.[3]

Sighele's *La Coppia criminale* is in part a detailed description, in part an explanation of this transformation. For Sighele, the particular character of the crowd was such that it cannot simply be seen as the sum of its parts. The behavior of the group as a whole is entirely different from what would be expected of each individual member acting alone.[4] The individuals united in a crowd are no longer what outward appearances suggest: a simple aggregate. The crowd must be viewed, Sighele says, as a definite entity, an individual itself, and this justifies the concept of a "crowd mind."

Seen from outside, the crowd is an unorganized multitude composed of heterogeneous elements and lacking structure and specialized parts.[5] This purely superficial appearance, which coincides closely with the ordinary person's perspective, is not the essence of the crowd phenomenon. The psychological characteristics of the crowd reveal its real nature; solving the problem of the crowd amounts to investigating the crowd mind. For Sighele and others of his school, the problem of the crowd was a social-psychological one. This meant a complete break with the methods of the Italian school of positive law from which Sighele's approach was derived, for the Italian school was able to attempt an explanation of crowd lawlessness only by subjecting the physical and mental characteristics of each individual in the crowd to anthropological investigations.[6]

It is difficult to draw a clear, unambiguous definition of "crowd

3 Sighele, *Psychologie des Auflaufs und der Massenverbrechen*, pp. 20ff.

4 Ibid., p. 44.

5 Ibid., p. 24; Tarde, *Philosophie pénale*, p. 320.

6 Lombroso and Lasche, *Der Politische Verbrecher*. Although Sighele's explanation of the crowd is guided by completely different principles, it is nevertheless interesting to note that he cannot completely free himself from the old concepts, for the assertion is made here that no complete explanation of crowd phenomena is possible without considering anthropological factors. See Sighele, *Psychologie des Auflaufs . . .*, p. 74.

mind" from Sighele and other writers of his school. Sighele's discussion of the crowd mind can be summarized in the principle: In the crowd, the intellectual abilities of individuals cancel out each other; on the other hand, their emotions are intensified through reciprocal interaction so that the entity formed is governed by a single feeling whose strength is the sum of the intensities of individual emotions.[7] This principle not only offers a description but also an explanation of crowds, including what Sighele saw as their instinctive criminal characteristics. (Instinct is used here as a psychological rather than a biological term, and includes all

[7] Sighele, *Psychologie des Auflaufs*, p. 201. "From an emotional standpoint, man is a cumulative being; he is not so intellectually. In other words, feelings can be added up; for thoughts there is only an arithmetical mean. Therefore a hundred courageous men make a heroically courageous aggregate, whereas a hundred brilliant men result in a group of only average intelligence. But the question of why the emotional qualities in a group behave so differently from the intellectual ones is not answered in this way. I would like to explain the fact that intellect and talent do not have the same suggestive powers as do feelings and emotions. One speaks of courage being infused, and that is very correct; the same is true of many other emotional gifts and failings: fear, hate, credulity, sympathy can be communicated precisely because they are acquired rather than inherited by the individual; not so with talent and intellect. One is born either with or without them, but he cannot acquire them. Admittedly, the moral qualities depend more on inheritance than on upbringing, which has always been emphasized by the positivistic school of criminal law; however, aside from exceptions, it is always easier to form a good person through upbringing and good example than it is to form an intellectually outstanding one. My remarks pertain not only to man, as he lives relatively separated in society, but also to groups of many people which suddenly occur. I'm speaking about the acute states of human groups, about riots, crowds, sects, not about the daily social community. The principle discussed can always be applied to these acute associations. That is evident and needs no proof. One only needs to observe any such group of people, and he will find that a shout, a gesture, a single word is able to bring them to the height of feeling or passion, but there is no event that could raise their intellectual level or transmit the spark of genuis to a thousand brains. Thus the intellectual facilities cannot be added together, because they cannot be communicated via suggestion, and this is so because they possess no external means of transmission." Compare Simmel, *Soziale Differenzierung*, p. 75.

those acts of volition accompanied by vague, indistinct ideas.) In the crowd, the only individual characteristics which persevere are those common to all individuals.[8] But precisely because the crowd is a mass of people with heterogeneous characteristics, the resulting crowd mind is formed from the lowest, most brutal characteristics of its individuals; in uncontrolled passion the crowd gives itself over to wild cruelty.[9]

Although Sighele's first work is limited to a study of crowd lawlessness, he does present certain general observations which can serve to explain other kinds of social groups as well. In his

8 Sighele, *Psychologie des Auflaufs*, p. 18. "One could say that all normal people possess certain characteristics which give them the same common quality, here called 'x.' A more talented person might possess in addition a higher quality called 'b'; another person, 'c'; another, 'd'; etc. As a result, in a group composed of 20 people—even if they were geniuses of the highest order—20 'x' would be present, but only one each of 'b,' 'c,' etc., that is, the common human factor possessed by all, would push back the individual personality, and the worker's cap would cover the doctor's and philosopher's hood. . . . In the groups discussed before (juries, committees, corporations), at least a certain key portion of those individuals composing them were in control. On the other hand are the collectivities brought together by pure chance, for example, the participants at a public meeting, spectators in a theater, people as they congregate in the streets and squares. Here the process reappears even more clearly. These conglomerations of people certainly do not manifest—everyone knows this, it is unnecessary to elaborate further—the psychology of the single individuals who compose them."

9 Ibid., p. 130. "In the confusion of men and voices, where no one commands and no one obeys, the wild emotions become as free as the noble ones, and unfortunately the heroes, who are not lacking, are powerless faced with the force of the murderers. The murderers are the ones who act; the majority, composed of irresolute atoms, stands without comprehension and without being able to resist."

Ibid., p. 206. "There is admittedly something disturbing in the conclusions to which I, along with Tarde, have come. Collectivities, whether they are called juries or committees, arrive at worse results morally and intellectually, than each single member would have produced. Thus whenever a person acts together with others, it means a lowering of his personal level. We have to accommodate ourselves to this result, and thus to a pessimistic formula." Compare Tarde, *Essais et mélanges sociologiques*, pp. 21ff.

later study, *La Delinquenza settaria,* Sighele attempted to apply principles from his first work to somewhat different material. In this book a new conception of the crowd is presented. The definition is more inclusive than before, when Sighele limited himself to the conspicuous phenomenon of the popular riot. Now the crowd appears as a generic notion under which are subsumed a whole series of secondary categories such as sect, caste, etc. The crowd is both the original and the general form of the human group. Historically, all forms of the group derive from the crowd, and seen genetically, they form an unbroken line of development from this nuclear form up to the state.[10]

However, along with this general concept of the crowd, the narrower definition reappears: the crowd as criminal mob, popular riot, rabble. In this narrower sense the crowd is differentiated from the sect. Crowd in the limited sense and sect are seen as special types of the generic concept of crowd. The difference between the two types lies in the fact that the sect is a "chronic form" of the crowd. The collective mood temporarily controls individuals in a crowd. If the mood continues for a longer time, so that individuals remain continually under the pressure of this dark common urging, then a sect exists.[11] Only the quality of transience differen-

10 Sighele, *Psychologie des sectes,* p. 41. "A shout, a fire, a bomb exploding in the street or on the fairgrounds, a derailment of a train; in a moment unorganized people become banded together for a common end; thus a simple physical proximity gives birth to a psychological union; thus, in a word, is created the crowd which can progress by an infinite series of degrees through the corporation up to the state.

"Today a crowd and a state ought to appear as two essentially distinct aggregates—as a matter of fact, they are—but the second can only be regarded as a remarkable development of the first. The modern state is indeed only the primtive and savage crowd transformed by centuries of history and social development. The state is an aggregate of men united by their view of a permanent, conscious, and general goal, while the crowd has a goal that is only ephemeral, unconscious, and particular. The state is a union of individuals whose supreme and necessary law is the division of labor and organization, but the crowd is an unorganized body where no one has his special part."

11 Ibid., p. 46. "The sect is a crowd which is selective and permanent. The crowd is a transitory sect which did not choose its members. The sect

tiates the crowd from the sect. Since the crowd is short-lived, it often seems preferable to speak of it as a phenomenon undergoing formation and dissolution rather than as a static entity.

This tendency to form two definitions of the crowd, one generic, the other specific, is of logical interest. It shows clearly how the need for a more exact definition made itself felt as empirical evidence increased. Sighele's extension of the crowd definition beyond the limits set in his first work points to the influence of Le Bon, who in *Psychologie des foules* (*The Crowd*) was the first to formulate the generic concept of the crowd.[12]

III

Gustave Le Bon's work presents a more systematic and less biased treatment of the crowd, for it is free from the prejudices which Sighele carried over from the Italian school of positive criminal law. In its essentials, however, Le Bon's definition of the crowd is the same as Sighele's. For both of them, a study of the crowd begins with the idea that the crowd cannot be seen as a simple aggregate, but is much more a collective entity whose unity is based on the special kind of mutual dependence among the individuals who compose it. With this definition, Le Bon rejects the usual meaning given to the term "crowd." In emphasizing the psychological aspect, that is, the reciprocity between individuals,

---

is an enduring form of the crowd; the crowd is the most intense form of the sect. . . . The sect is thus the first crystallization of any doctrine. Out of the confused and amorphous state in which it is manifested in the crowd, every idea is expected to specify itself in the well-defined form of the sect, unless it later becomes a party, a school, or a scientific, political, or spiritual religion. . . . It is the first stage in which the human group, leaving the amorphous state of the undefinable, variable, and anonymous crowd, arrives at a definition and an integration which will subsequently lead to the highest and most perfect human group: the state."

12 Ibid., p. 43. "First of all, one can observe that giving the name crowd to any human group whatsoever is incorrect. And from the grammatical point of view, this opinion seems indisputable to me. With more precision, Tarde distinguishes associations and corporations from crowds."

he assigns a purely theoretical meaning to the word "crowd" (*foule*).[13]

Le Bon sees certain conditions under which an aggregate of people takes on characteristics that are new and different from those of one man alone. Under such conditions the totality becomes an entity, or as Le Bon calls it, a psychological crowd (*foule psychologique*). Crowd used in this sense differs from the normal meaning of the word in that the usual spatial aspect is ignored. A number of individuals gathered in a square constitutes a crowd in Le Bon's sense only when it possesses a certain psychological nature.[14] On the other hand, an entire nation can be a crowd in the psychological sense, without any visible gathering of people. Thus it is the psychological conditions rather than the spatial relationships of individuals which form the essential content of the concept "crowd."[15]

What are these psychological states in individuals, which can be seen as the characteristics of a group, sociologically defined? Le Bon specifies two:

1. The disappearance of all individual and particular self-consciousness in members of the group. This submergence of the individual in the crowd is actually the same thing as the emergence of the instincts and commonly shared attributes which serve to define the life of the species.

2. The feelings and thoughts of all the crowd members move in the same direction. These two attributes have been combined by Le Bon into one general concept which he calls the collective mind. A gathering of people can only be called a crowd in the sociological

13 Gustave Le Bon, *Psychologie des foules*, pp. 11ff.

14 Ibid., p. 12. "A thousand individuals accidentally united in a public square without any determined goal does not at all constitute a psychological crowd. . . . At certain moments, a half dozen men can constitute a psychological crowd, whereas hundreds of men united by chance might not constitute one. On the other hand, an entire nation, without having visible connections, can become a crowd under the action of certain influences."

15 Le Bon, *Psychologie des foules*, pp. 12, 13; Sighele, *Psychologie des sectes*, p. 40; Tarde, *L'Opinion et la foule*, p. 167. Compare Lazarus and Steinthal, *Zeitschrift für Völkerpsychologie*, 1:11.

sense when the self-consciousness of all individual members of the group is so merged that the result appears as a new entity: a common consciousness. Then the collectivity has become a crowd, sociologically speaking.[16] What existed as a heterogeneous mass under previous conditions is transformed into a homogeneous entity.

(Le Bon applied the concept "collective mind" in different ways according to context. He not only speaks of collective and crowd mind, but also of national mind. Regardless of how the meaning of these terms might differ or coincide throughout his works, it is clear that the basic concept includes the two characteristics mentioned above, and has no additional meaning.[17])

This merging of everything that is individual and particular explains for Le Bon the fact that the crowd is never able to undertake anything requiring a high degree of intelligence.[18] The crowd has at its disposal only those limited attributes which every member possesses to the same degree.[19]

The newest proponent of collective psychology is Pasquale

16 Le Bon, *Psychologie des foules*, p. 20. "Thus the disappearance of the conscious personality, the dominance of the unconscious personality, orientation of feelings and ideas in the same direction through suggestion and contagion, a tendency to transform suggested ideas immediately into action; these then are the principal characteristics of the individual in the crowd." See also Sighele, *Psychologie des sectes*, pp. 80, 85, 139.

17 Le Bon, *Les Lois psychologiques de l'évolution des peuples*, p. 11; *Psychologie du socialisme*, pp. 61, 62, 71; *Psychologie des foules*, pp. 68, 72, 132.

18 Le Bon, *Psychologie des foules*, p. 17. "It is exactly this possession in common of ordinary qualities which explains why crowds are never able to accomplish acts which demand a higher degree of intelligence. Decisions made in their own common interest by a group of distinguished men who come however from different specialties, are not perceptibly superior to decisions made by a gathering of imbeciles. When working together, they are only able to use those average qualities which they all possess in common. In crowds, it is the stupidities and not the intellect which add to each other."

19 The intellectual weakness of the group has already drawn the attention of other writers. Compare Tarde, *L'Opinion et la foule*, p. 180; Sighele, *Psychologie des sectes*, p. 190; Sighele, *Psychologie des Auflaufs*, p. 26; Lombroso, *Die Anarchisten*, p. 19.

Rossi. In a series of works he has carried further the concepts of Le Bon and Sighele, so that the crowd now appears as the prototypical form of association itself. For Rossi, the kinds of crowds form a developmental series beginning with the lowest, most undifferentiated and impermanent kinds—those called crowds in everyday speech—and ending with the highest, most differentiated and permanent one, the state.[20] Between these extremes lie all the groups mentioned previously, such as sect, class, etc. The principle of classification is that of progressive social differentiation and increasing stability from stage to stage.[21] This principle is identical with the general evolutionary law of Herbert Spencer,[22] but the application is new. In a strict sense, it is no longer a law of evolution, but a principle of classification. However, it must be remembered that this classification is a psychological one. According to Rossi, the difference between collective psychology and sociology is that collective psychology is concerned with the collective mind, and sociology with the physical structure, the body, of human association.

In Rossi's works, the study of crowd psychology seems to grow beyond its boundaries. Here the teachings of collective psychology find their boldest and most inclusive expression. Outside this school, the question of the crowd is only occasionally discussed, and such descriptions generally agree with those of Le Bon.[23]

20 Pasquale Rossi, *L'Animo della folla*, p. 4. "The crowd can be defined as an unstable and undifferentiated formation, evolving within the sphere of a stable and differentiated aggregate (city, town, village). . . . From this primitive form of a crowd, essentially unstable and undifferentiated, one passes to other forms more stable and differentiated. The evolution which is valid for social organisms here also involves a growing differentiation and an increasing integration."

21 Ibid., p. 12. "The last, and the most differentiated form of a crowd, is the state, a stable form that now is a power of mediation among different classes or among the various divisions of one class. Now it is the political organ of one class only. . . . The crowd, the caste, the class, the state, the sect, are really forms of evolution, links in a chain of which the first is the crowd and the last is the state."

22 Compare Gaupp, *Herbert Spencer*, p. 93.

23 Sighele, *Psychologie des sectes*, pp. 41, 196, 192; Tarde, *L'Opinion et la foule*, p. 167; Baldwin, *Social and Ethical Interpretations in Mental*

What distinguishes the crowd psychology approach is its emphasis on the merging of individuals into one entity as the essential characteristic of the social group. The resulting crowd is seen as a new sentient individual, a collective being different from its component members.

IV

Once the crowd is viewed as a new collective being, its characteristics can be considered. The individuals who compose a crowd exhibit different characteristics, depending upon whether they are acting alone or are united in the crowd. Those traits peculiar to individuals when they were united in a crowd were called "crowd characteristics" by Le Bon.

As Le Bon sees them, these crowd characteristics are:

1. Heightened emotional sensitivity, impetuosity and capriciousness. The individual by himself can be subjected to the same stimuli as the man in a crowd, but the individual's intellect makes him alert to the results of his actions, and he suppresses the dangerous impulses. "The individual," Le Bon states, "can direct his reflexes, while the crowd is incapable of doing this."[24] Since very different kinds of stimuli can affect crowds, and crowds unfailingly react to them, it follows that a crowd is very capricious. This explains how a crowd's bloodthirsty cruelty can change in an instant into generosity or unbounded heroism.

2. Increased suggestibility and credulity. The crowd yields to all suggestions. It has no critical sense, and as a result exhibits extreme credulity. The most incredible myths and legends can arise and spread in a crowd.[25]

3. Exaggerated and one-sided opinions. The crowd, "like women," moves directly to extremes. The mere mention of a

---

Development, pp. 245ff.; Sidis, *Psychology of Suggestion*, p. 304; Sighele, *Psychologie des Auflaufs*, p. 28. Compare Dr. M. Campeano, *Essais de psychologie militaire, individuelle et collective;* Pasquale Rossi, *La Psicologia collettiva morbosa.*

24 Le Bon, *Psychologie des foules*, p. 25.

25 Ibid., p. 28.

suspicion results in its immediate acceptance as incontestable fact. In the crowd, the simple or ignorant person loses his feelings of insignificance which are replaced by the idea of unlimited power.

4. This leads to another crowd characteristic: intolerance and despotism.[26] The crowd is as domineering as it is intolerant. The individual can listen to argument and opposition, but the crowd never can. In public gatherings, the slightest opposition offered by a speaker is received with shouts. If the speaker insists on sticking to his views, loud cries demand that he be thrown out.

5. The final "crowd characteristic" which is evident is: personal distinterestedness or unselfishness.[27] The crowd is more capable of sacrifice and unselfish acts than the individual. While personal interest only rarely serves as a strong motivating force for the person acting in the crowd, the reverse is almost exclusively the case with individuals acting alone.[28]

It is easy to explain these so-called "crowd characteristics" of heightened sensitivity, credulity, intolerance, etc. They are all only different expressions of one emotional state which is generated by the reciprocal influence of individual emotions and which affects all members of the crowd in the same way. As a result of the entire process by which the crowd comes into being, an expectant motor attitude is created, that is, a state of suggestibility often so pronounced that it has been compared with that of hypnosis.[29] This state of suggestibility can be viewed as a crowd condition not only because it affects all members of the group in the same way, but even more because it depends on the reciprocal influences of the

26 Ibid., pp. 38, 39.
27 Ibid., p. 41.
28 Ibid., pp. 45, 46.
29 Sidis, *The Psychology of Suggestion*, p. 327. "Social suggestibility is individual hypnotism written large. The laws of hypnosis work on a great scale in society. Hypnotic suggestion is especially effective if it accords with the character of the subject. The same holds true in the case of social hypnotization. Each nation has its own bent of mind, and suggestions given in that direction are fatally effective. The Jew is a fair example. Religious emotions are at the base of his character and he is also highly suggestible to religious suggestions."

individuals on one another. Thus the term "crowd suggestion" is used.[30]

V

If an attempt is made to form a complete picture of everything written about the crowd, it becomes evident that certain scientific motives have influenced the formation of the crowd concept. These motives must be examined in order to understand thoroughly the concept and its scientific meaning.[31]

As first used by the school of crowd psychology, the term "crowd" meant the same as popular riot, but this is not a scientific definition. Whenever the word appears in everyday usage, its applications and nuances are so broad and varied that they preclude one clear and unambiguous definition of the concept. The most precise meaning of the word refers to a gathering of a number of individuals in one place. If so used, a crowd would be like a pile of stones, nothing more than a number of mutually independent individuals who either appear to the eye, or are at least mentally perceived as one actual unit. Such a unit based only on the spatial relationship of its parts and not on their reciprocal influences is not a real unit, since it is precisely the dynamic reciprocity of its parts which constitutes the essence of the whole.[32]

30 Stoll, *Suggestions und Hypnotismus in der Völkerpsychologie* [n. p.]. "There are above all two characteristics of the suggestive process which are important in the psychology of national character [*Völkerpsychologie*].

"The first is the ease with which suggestive illusions can be aroused in a large number of completely awake people. The second is the enormous contagiousness of certain suggestions, that is, the possibility of imparting one and the same suggestion to a whole crowd of people; thus Crowd Suggestion, or '*Suggestion collective*' of the French."

31 Rickert, *Die Grenzen der Naturwissenschaftlichen Begriffsbildung*, chap. 1.

32 Kistiakowski, *Gesellschaft und Einzelwesen*, pp. 114ff. "All these entities (forests, mountains, and animal societies such as herds and swarms) exist as more than logical constructions and do not simply have a conceptual origin. In contrast, other collective terms, which are

Because of this essence or uniformity based on internal relationships, a unit can be the object of scientific study. The material investigated by each exact science consists of objects composed of parts which are in dynamic relationship to one another and the procedure common to all explanatory sciences entails separating a thing into its parts. Out of their relationships, then, the essence of the whole—that is, the uniform processes of its formation, dissolution, and other behavior—can be derived and formulated into laws.[33]

Thus it becomes clear that crowd psychology must form a new concept of its object in order to explain the crowd phenomenon. This concept must present the whole as a unit determined by the essential relationships of its constitutent parts. Here the approach of collective psychology diverges from popular notions. For explanatory science, spatial juxtaposition cannot serve as the essential characteristic of the crowd.[34] Individuals can be designated a crowd not because they are together, but because they mutually infect each other with their thoughts and feelings.

Common experience demonstrates that people under the in-

---

only artificial categories of similar things or processes, simply comprise spatial and temporal coincidence of certain facts. These can only be viewed as numerical aggregates; repetition of certain of their characteristics forms the only basis of using them as conceptual entities."

33 Rickert, *Grenzen*, p. 212. "If we want to employ the word [nature] as a precise term in science, then we will have to say that nature represents reality as uniformly recurring relationships."

Ibid., p. 129. "Thus we will apply the word 'explanation' for a particular kind of understanding; with this we intend to say that a scientific explanation only exists where a phenomenon has been subsumed under a concept; this concept must have reached the third stage. That is, it not only is a definition or a compilation of characteristics, but it expresses an essential relationship, i.e., a natural law of universal application. When this is achieved, we have a so-called 'causal' explanation, that is, we know whenever this general concept can be applied, why something is or behaves the way it does."

34 Ibid., p. 67. "We know that the prerequisite for the broadest application of the scientific concept is its freedom from spatial and temporal determinants, so that it can be applied to every form of reality regardless of the temporal and spatial expression such reality assumes."

fluence of a collective stimulus often carry out actions which as individuals they neither could nor would do. Writers of the collective psychology school frequently employ the maxim: "Senatores boni viri; senatus autem mala bestia." It is indeed the popular riot's tendency to irrational rage and its blind destructive spirit exceeding all individual passions that first captured the attention of collective psychology.[35] The equally characteristic ability of the crowd to accomplish heroic acts that none of the individual members would have the courage to attempt alone was first stressed by Le Bon. His emphasis on this fact suggests that he considered an individual capable of heroism only when acting under the influence of crowd excitement.[36]

It must be concluded that the suggestive influence exerted by people on each other constitutes the deciding characteristic of the crowd; and the social epidemic becomes the typical social phenomenon for collective psychology.[37] It appears that mental or emotional states combine in a direct causal relationship and their interaction gives rise to a general excitement which controls the group as a unit. The great classic examples of crowds are that last

35 Sidis, *The Psychology of Suggestion*, p. 304. "In my article, 'A Study of the Mob,' I point out that the mob has a self of its own; that the personal self is suppressed, swallowed up by it, so much so that when the latter comes once more to the light of day it is frequently horrified at the work, the crime, the mob self had committed; and that once the mob self is generated, or, truer to say, brought to the surface, it possesses a strong attractive power, and a great capacity for assimilation. It attracts fresh individuals, breaks down their personal life, and quickly assimilates them; it effects in them a disaggregation of consciousness and assimilates the sub-waking selves. *Out of the sub-waking selves the mob self springs into being.* The assimilated individual expresses nothing but the energy suggestion, the will of the entranced crowd; he enters freely into the spirit of the mob."

36 Le Bon, *Psychologie des foules*, p. 45. "Only collectivities are capable of great unselfishness and great devotion."

37 Sidis, *Psychology of Suggestion*, pp. 310–11. "Man is a social animal, no doubt, but *he is social because he is suggestible.* Blind obedience is a social virtue. But blind obedience is the very essence of suggestibility, the constitution of the disaggregated sub-waking self. Society by its nature, by its organization, tends to run riot in mobs, manias, crazes and all kinds of mental epidemics."

vast migration of peoples, the Crusades, and the French Revolution. They serve as examples of the spatial and temporal effects of the social epidemic. Here the crowd appears as a great revolutionary force which shakes and overturns a whole civilization.

Examples of the suggestive influence exerted by people on one another occur in all realms of social life. So viewed, the phenomena known in different places during the fourteenth and fifteenth centuries as St. Johannes's and St. Vitus's dance are highly interesting. Incidentally, this late medieval rage for dancing was not a new phenomenon but was already well known in the Middle Ages.[38] Similarities to the medieval dance mania are found in the exuberance of the bacchanal dance festivals of antiquity and in the way in which they spread like an epidemic throughout Greece in spite of much resistance. A recent book by Stoll demonstrates that this "crowd suggestion" not only appears in isolated instances throughout social life, but has played a great role everywhere in the life of primitive as well as civilized man.[39] It is because of this widespread occurrence of crowd suggestion that collective psychology can claim the status of an explanatory social science.

VI

One difficulty now becomes evident: since emotional contagion is such a general phenomenon, it is not clear how the boundaries between social groups are to be drawn. If the crowd phenomenon coincides with that of social suggestion, then it seems that the crowd must be viewed as a simple emotional state controlling a number of individuals, a mood whose limits are as difficult to delineate as those of the weather. In that case, physical existence [*Substantialität*] could hardly be listed as one of the

38 Rohde, *Psyche, Seelenkult und Unsterblichkeitsglaube der Griechen*, p. 325.

39 Stoll, *Suggestion und Hypnotismus*, [n. p.]. Cf. Hecker, *Die Tanzwut, eine Volkskrankheit im Mittelalter; Der Schwarze Tod im 14. Jahrhundert;* and *Kinderfahrt, eine Historische Pathologische Skizze;* Förstemann, *Die Christliche Geisslergesellschaft;* Yandell, "Epidemic Convulsions," *Brain*, vol. 4, 1881–82, [n. p.]; Regnard, *Les Maladies épidémiques de l'esprit;* Friedmann, *Ueber Wahnideen im Völkerleben;* v. Bechterew, *Suggestion und ihre soziale Bedeutung.*

crowd's characteristics. Instead, the crowd itself would have to be viewed as a characteristic of something else.

Everyone lives continually in this atmosphere of social suggestion, inasfar as a person's feelings and thoughts are always influenced and defined to some degree by the feelings and thoughts of others. At every encounter emotional and mental contact is experienced. Every occasion, whether a marriage or a funeral, has its own peculiar mood which controls the feelings of those present. Two individuals sit down at the table and begin to speak with each other. Regardless of how far apart they are from agreeing, a common bond immediately develops which affects both of them to the same degree. A third person sits down with them; now the mood changes and a new one develops. This process of reciprocal action and psychic adjustment occurs continually and automatically wherever people are together. People are usually not conscious of the influence of these social forces surrounding them; awareness occurs only when passing from one social situation into another or when the psychic atmosphere is suddenly disrupted. From this viewpoint, the crowd would seem to be a simple stirring of the psychic atmosphere, a disturbance of the social equilibrium.

There is no question that a real difficulty presents itself whenever a serious attempt is made to define "crowd." The same conceptual vagueness is again apparent in the ambiguous descriptions of crowd types used by different writers. Although Le Bon employs crowd as a generic concept including the most varied kinds of social groups, he nevertheless makes a clear distinction between crowd and nationality.[40] Tarde uses the concept of crowd in a

40 Le Bon, *Psychologie des foules*, p. 143. Le Bon has classified the crowd in the following manner:
Heterogeneous crowds:

1. Anonymous (crowds gathered on the street, etc.).
2. Nonanonymous (juries, parliamentary assemblies, etc.).

Homogeneous crowds:

1. Sects (political, religious, etc.).
2. Castes (military, priestly, working castes, etc.).
3. Classes (bourgeoisie, peasantry, etc.).

Relative to the relationship of crowd to nationality, compare Le Bon, ibid., pp. 67ff., and *Les Lois psychologiques de l'évolution des peuples* [n. p.].

much narrower sense than Le Bon and other writers. He differentiates, for example, between crowd and public and does not include the sect as a particular kind of crowd.[41] Sighele stands between Tarde and Le Bon, defining the crowd first in a narrower, and later in a wider sense. Rossi differs from the others in stating that the crowd and the social group are essentially identical. But in spite of these differences, all the writers of this school insist on one assumption: the defining characteristic of the crowd is not spatial juxtaposition, but the presence of psychic reciprocity.

However, reciprocity alone does not constitute the essence of the crowd. Whenever suggestive reciprocity reaches a certain degree of intensity, the people involved are caught up so strongly in emotional and mental currents that they are swept along, as if caught in a flood, towards an unknown goal. This shows how certain individuals cut themselves loose from society and join together around a new nucleus of feelings and ideas. In the final analysis it is such a psychic current, together with the individuals carried by it, to which collective psychology has given the name "crowd."[42]

What is essential in this conception of the crowd is not only the fact that here the feelings and desires of a number of people are reciprocally modified, promoted, and inhibited. Also important is that the entire process bears upon one and the same goal; the resulting unity is teleological. This is what is meant when collective psychology attributes a mind to the crowd. In it resides the real existence of the group.

41 Tarde, *L'Opinion et la foule*, pp. 1ff., and p. 202. "A crowd, even when the majority is made up of good people, can easily be led to kinds of passionate crimes, to fits of instantaneous homicidal alienation; while a sect, animated by strong and deeply rooted feeling, only commits rational and calculated crimes that always conform to its collective character and are strongly marked by the stamp of its race."

42 Ibid., p. 175. "Seen from the same view, all the tumultuous gatherings which precede the outbreak of mutiny and which are intimately related to each other—the habitual phenomena of revolutionary crises—can be considered as one and the same crowd. They belong in the category of complex crowds, a series of group waves."

2

THE SOCIOLOGICAL PROCESS

I

WHEN sociology is viewed not as the philosophy of history, as is commonly the case,[1] but more as the embodiment of all descriptive and explanatory social science, a certain unique logical difficulty exists which is not encountered in other natural sciences.[2] This difficulty is that sociology's subject matter, the social group, is not perceived by the senses as a physical unit. To the naive perception, the social group appears simply as a number of spatially separate individuals whose independence from one another is accepted without question. From this it is clear that what other sciences take for granted, namely the unity and concreteness of their subject matter, becomes itself a problem for sociology.

Scientific activity usually begins with the description and classification of objects, such as trees, people, stones, etc., to which simple perception attributes a physical oneness and a concrete

1 Compare Paul Barth, *Die Philosophie der Geschichte als Soziologie*, Foreword, p. 4. "To me, history appears as concrete sociology, just as a drama is concrete characterology. A theory of history, however, will necessarily be abstract, and will be identical with abstract sociology." See also ibid., pp. 4ff.

2 In this study we will proceed from the methodological contrast between history and natural science as it is found in Windelband ("Geschichte und Naturwissenschaft," Chancellor's Address, Strassbourg, 1894), and also in Rickert, *Die Grenzen*.

Compare also Simmel, *Die Probleme der Geschichtsphilosophie;* Münsterberg, *Grundzüge der Psychologie*, pp. 133ff.; Kistiakowski, *Gesellschaft und Einzelwesen*, pp. 42ff.

and unchanging form. Under closer observation, this apparently concrete and real form may be seen to actually exist in a state of permanent change. If this is the case, then an attempt is made to preserve its substantiality by first separating the object into its parts. These parts are then viewed as concrete and unchanging things; their oneness appears as a fundamental principle by which the changing relationships of the parts are defined. The substantiality of the object is thus seen in terms of the law governing the mutual relationship of its parts.[3]

Sociology, in contrast, cannot proceed in this manner because the social group does not exist as a real entity, but must be transformed into one. Social relationships can be understood causally; they depict reciprocal actions which can eventually be expressed in laws. Once this is understood, the social group can be spoken of as a real entity, that is, it can become the object to be scientifically explained.[4]

Collective psychology, for example, assumes that the unity of the group resides in the unity of its actions, so that the group can be seen as a functional unity. At this point the old question arises in a new form: what is the physical basis of the group? It is precisely here that the problem of sociology reveals itself in its most puzzling form. The difficulty lies in the fact that the same individuals appear as members of different groups. A, B, C and D, for example, are all members of the stock exchange and all of them also belong to the same social club. It appears that the same physical base is shared by two completely different social structures whose interests and traditions are totally different.

Just as the members are incapable of serving as the physical basis of a group, so are the cultural institutions of which they make use. The difficulties here become clear upon considering that cultural institutions—especially tools, instruments, and machines such as the railroad, telegraph, and printing press, etc.—can only be regarded as an "extension of the sensory-motor response system," as separable parts of the individual's psycho-physical

3 Compare Sigwart, *Logik*, vol. 2, secs. 76–79.
4 Kistiakowski, *Gesellschaft und Einzelwesen*, pp. 111ff.

mechanisms.[5] Precisely because these cultural institutions are shared by all individuals and all groups indiscriminately, they cannot be used to physically differentiate one social group from the other.

It would be better to seek the physical basis of the group in the brain and the physiology of the nervous system. It is known that when any one of the motor systems in the brain is stimulated, all the others are more or less inhibited. The assumption follows that where individuals work together there must develop in each one of them a particular motor system that is related to the parallel motor systems of all other individuals in the group. This would result in a common motor system such as that seen, for example, among football players where each movement of the one individual calls forth a corresponding movement in all the others. Insofar as this common motor system inhibits all other possible motor systems, the corresponding total structure could be thought of as the physical basis of the group.[6]

Although the physical basis of the group can be theoretically

5 Münsterberg, *Grundzüge*, p. 477. "The tool, in the widest imaginable sense of the word, is an extension of the sensory-motor response system, an extension which is mechanically separate from the organism, but belongs to it biologically, like the shell to the shellfishes and snails. It is important for the sociologist that man creates the tool for his goals according to his plans; the biologist sees in this planning and creating an activity of the brain and thus a physical function through which the tool itself becomes a bodily product. That the material from which the tool is made is not a bodily secretion, but comes from material existing outside it, may be physiologically important, but is biologically of secondary importance. Thus, there is biologically no difference between a spider's web and a bird's nest; in one case the material remains outside the body, in the other case it has gone through the body and has been transformed via a vegetative process."

6 Bosanquet, *The Philosophical Theory of the State*, pp. 173ff: "Every individual mind, then, so far as it takes part in social groupings or institutions, is a structure of appercipient systems, answering, each to each, to the different capacities in which it enters into each grouping respectively."

Ibid., p. 175. "The social whole, regarded from a corresponding point of view, would be a whole consisting of psychical dispositions and their activities, answering to one another in determinate ways."

defined in this way, in practice no one would attempt to apply such a definition in detail. To do so would demonstrate that the social group cannot be defined as a physical entity in this manner, although the attempt might ultimately bring forth a description and explanation of the group that make use of physiological concepts. At the same time it would become clear that as soon as sociology no longer merely describes the forms of relationships in which social life is expressed, but attempts instead to explain social forms and life, it necessarily becomes social psychology.[7]

The same problem emerges in the question: what are the basic units with which sociology is concerned? It has been established that the process common to all explanatory sciences consists of resolving an object into its parts so that the totality can be explained from their relationships. Each explanatory science reserves only a part of empirical reality as its subject matter, or at least views empirical reality from a particular standpoint. And within its area of research, each science attempts to resolve things into the parts which it regards as the smallest analyzable units.

A logical classification of the different natural sciences can now be projected, differentiating them according to: (1) their particular basic units, (2) the kind of interaction occurring between such units.[8] In physics the basic unit is the physical atom, and the general form of the interaction between atoms is expressed in the law of gravitation. On the other hand, the basic unit of chemistry is more concrete than that of physics; that is, compared with atoms, the basic units of chemistry exhibit more properties, are more self-determinate, and in their mutual relations show a greater diversity even though they remain fully definable to science. In chemistry the analysis of units as relationships is not reduced as far as it is in physics, which explains why the basic unit in chemistry is considered more concrete than that of physics. Turning to

7 Simmel, "Das Problem der Soziologie," *Jahrbuch für Gesetzgebung*, XVII, 4, p. 1301; Münsterberg, *Grundzüge*, p. 133.

8 Rickert, *Die Grenzen*, p. 125. "Natural science not only juxtaposes characteristics in order to define the contents of a concept, but rather it collects a number of elements which belong together and thus embarks upon concept formation which is capable of ultimately developing concepts which implicitly contain general judgments or natural laws."

biology, the basic unit is even more concrete, more self-determinate. The cell possesses, for example, characteristics which enable it to (1) reproduce itself and (2) adapt itself to its environment. The interaction of these basic units and their mutual adaptation, division of function, etc., provide a basis for attempting to explain the living organism.[9]

It becomes apparent that if this logical ordering were feasible, sciences would form an ascending series, with every higher stage related to a more concrete basic unit.[10] This does not mean that the subject matter governed by the laws of any given science is not affected by the laws of all sciences lower in order and more abstract. Rather, the lower systems are prerequisities to the existence of each higher one. The new, more concrete basic unit makes it possible to abstract from all those relationships—which is precisely the concern of the more abstract sciences. Thus, while the cell can be explained physically and chemically, biology does not explain it,

9 Ibid., p. 282. "On the other hand, however, biology also reveals an aspect which is scientific in our meaning of the word. Even where the scientific descriptive method is abandoned, one is not limited to presenting the history of the organism, but attempts instead to find the laws to which its life conforms, or at least to form concepts which are meant to be valid wherever organisms are present. Abstraction must take place, if not from the historical character of the various types, then at least from living specimens. Science may proceed, for example, to trace back the fullness of continually changing forms to processes. As organic processes they must always remain historically relative from the standpoint of a general theory of the material world; but compared to the continually changing forms of individual organisms they must be viewed as something permanent and unchanging. The concern, then, is the same as in physics and chemistry. Biology seeks nature within the historical process in order to become a natural science in the full sense of the word."

10 With the designation of various sciences as higher or lower ordered, any limitation on the independence of the various sciences is not intended. Likewise, this ordering is not at all to be seen as value relationship; seen from a logical standpoint, the science here designated as lower is actually regarded as higher, because the theoretical concerns of the more basic sciences are the most completely developed.

Compare Münsterberg, *Grundzüge*, p. 298. "To understand the object as a complex of component parts is a transformation whose goal must be an ordering of the object into a relationship of cause and effects; this transformation stands scientifically 'higher,' the more inclusive the relationship which is revealed by the analysis."

but treats it as the basic unit whose essence cannot be further reduced. Physiological chemistry, in contrast, would have regarded the cell as precisely the problem to be investigated.

Advancing to sociology, the basic unit can be expected to be still more concrete than it is in biology; here the individual himself can almost be regarded as this unit. This assumption actually exists in classical English political economy, where the individual is equated with the physical atom as a uniform and unchangeable unit. The difference is that while the atom remains bound in external relationships and is completely incapable of self-determination, the individual as seen by English political economy acts with absolute freedom, guided only by his drive for self-preservation.[11]

Contrary to the premises of political economy, it is known that

11 W. Hasbach, *Die allgemeinen philosophischen Grundlagen der von Quesnay und Adam Smith begründeten politischen Oekonomie*, p. 141. "The method of Hobbes receives its necessary supplementation through Cartesian psychology; now it is complete. Ricardo later utilized it in such a virtuoso manner that his work became a theory of economic life, and thus made possible a completely mathematical treatment of our science. It was the goal to which this trend necessarily led. The mathematician Descartes and Hobbes had introduced a method related to mathematics into the arts; and through the genius of men like Cauard, Conmot, Gossen, Walras, Jevons, the mathematics which had been latent was set free." Compare Bonar, *Philosophy and Political Economy*.

Lange, *Geschichte des Materialismus*, 2:451. "This mistake [that the followers of Adam Smith confused the laws of the market with the foundations of human behavior] contributed incidentally to giving political economy a strong scientific facade; it resulted in a considerable simplification of all problems of commerce. This simplification consisted of presenting man as completely egoistic, a being capable of fully realizing his particular interests without being inhibited by any other sentiments."

Bagehot, "The Postulates of Political Economy," *Economic Studies*, pp. 5ff. "More competent persons, indeed, have understood that English Political Economists are not speaking of real men, but of imaginary ones; not of men as we see them, but of men as it is convenient for us to suppose they are. But even they often do not understand that the world which our Political Economists treat of, is a very limited and peculiar world also. They often imagine that what they read is applicable to all states of society, and to all equally, whereas it is true only of—and only proved as to—states of society in which commerce has largely developed, and where it has taken the form of development, or something near the form, which it has taken in England."

people's interests are not always tied to their own physical well-being. The error of the opposite view arises from the psychological approach, which always draws parallels between psychic and physiological processes. Actually, a person's "self-interest" is tied to everything for which he decides to feel responsible, whether it is his children, his possessions, the outcome of his activities, or even the destiny of his immortal soul. Furthermore, these "self-interests" are so varied and often so contradictory that the empirical self cannot be said to possess a single self-identity. Instead, the empirical self is always changing, and is never self-consistent.[12] This means that the individual cannot be viewed as a basic unit; both from the above standpoint and in terms of the systems of relationships investigated by sociology, the individual does not constitute a permanent uniformity.

When collective psychology and political economy are compared, their initial propositions, at least, appear clearly opposed. Whereas for political economy egoistic individuals represent the basic units composing society, collective psychology does not regard the individual as a psychic entity: that is, his behavior is not transmitted and determined by self-awareness but instead reacts directly, quasi-instinctively, to its object. The respective premises of collective psychology and classical English political economy can both be justified within their area of concern and in view of the different interests they represent. But there still remains the possibility, even the necessity, of constructing a science with a perspective capable of including both approaches.[13]

12 James, *Psychology*, 1:291ff. Bosanquet, *Psychology of the Moral Self*, p. 47.

13 Lange, *Geschichte des Materialismus*, 2:455. "Admittedly, the abstracting of egoism [in behavior] is much stronger in political economy than in any other previous science, where both the contradictory influences of inertia and custom, and those of sympathy and sense of community are of utmost importance. Nevertheless, abstraction may be freely used, as long as it remains a conscious process. For if it is first discovered how those moving atoms in a hypothetical society adopting egoism would have to behave according to the premises, then not only would the abstraction be validated, which in itself is almost impossible to contradict, but also exact knowledge would be gained about one side of human essence and its elements, which plays a very important role in society, especially in business in general."

The beginnings of such a science are found in the so-called "imitation theory" encountered in various forms in French and American writings. In France, for example, Tarde has criticized the psychological concepts and premises of the old theories of political economy; his intention is to shift the perspective of economics from that of the individual to that of social psychology.[14] The American, Baldwin, has attempted to explain that sociological interaction is responsible for producing not only the group but also the sentient individual, that is, the individual viewed as an empirical personality.[15]

This clearly indicates that neither Baldwin nor Tarde viewed the individual himself as the basic unit in sociology. Baldwin as well as Royce tended to see the individual more as the outcome of the social process. This again illustrates how different writers could not agree on the basic unit: Tarde saw it as wishes and beliefs, while Baldwin claimed that ideas should constitute these basic units.[16] This author believes that the disagreement between

14 Compare Tarde, *Psychologie economique.*

15 Baldwin, *Social and Ethical Interpretations*, pp. 13ff; Royce, "Observations on Anomalies of Self Consciousness," *Psychological Review* 2, no. 5: [n. p.].

16 For the sociological basic unit, compare Tarde, *Études de psychologie sociale*, pp. 41ff.; *Les Lois de l'imitation*, pp. 1ff.; *La Logique sociale*, pp. 12ff.; and *L'Opposition universelle*, p. 339, where he writes: "The basic psychological units are beliefs and desires, insofar as they move or are capable of moving, within the same individual, from one group of sensations or images to another without being basically altered. The basic sociological units are beliefs and desires insofar as they are communicated or are communicable from one individual to other individuals, without changing their nature. When belief accumulates within the individual, it becomes conviction; when it spreads and intensifies in crowds, it assumes the name of truth."

Baldwin, *Social and Ethical Interpretations*, p. 505. "It is only thoughts or knowledge which are imitable in the fruitful way required by a theory of progressive social organization. It has been said by some that beliefs and desires are thus imitable. It is clear, however, to the psychologists that beliefs and desires are functions of the knowledge-contents about which they arise. No belief can be induced in one individual by another except as the fact, truth, information believed is first induced. The imitator must first get the thought before he can imitate belief in the

the two writers arises from a certain difference in their viewpoint, which will be taken up later. The fundamental units of sociology are here understood to be the volitional attitudes (willattitudes) [*Willenshaltungen*] of individuals interacting in a group situation. These attitudes can either be expressed as feelings (wishes and beliefs) or as conscious ideas.

Finally it must be emphasized that sociological unity is not identical with any definite physical oneness. Discrete individuals, along with all the social institutions through which they interact, compose a large psycho-physical mechanism; but this in itself does not create a sociological unity. Sociological unity is instead the functional unity which is performed through this mechanism.

II

There is nothing new about the notion that man, as one of the objects in the external world has a very special meaning for his fellow men, and that it is in the nature of man to react differently toward other humans than toward objects. This view was held by the Stoics and was introduced into modern philosophy as part of the moral-legal teachings of the Renaissance.[17] During the English Enlightenment this view reappeared in the idea of man's "original moral state" and provided a contrast to Hobbes's theory which states that man's value to his fellow men is no higher than the value of other useful objects of nature. For Hobbes as well as for Locke, the basis of all moral behavior lies outside human nature, namely, in authority.[18]

Another theory gradually developed which was closely allied to the doctrine of a natural social instinct prompting the expression of man's social nature. Proceeding from a deeper and more

---

thought. So of a desire, I cannot desire what you do except as I think of the desirable object somewhat as you do. Both belief and desire are, as has been argued above, functions of thought-content."

17 Windelband, *Die Geschichte der neuren Philosophie*, 1:269ff; Bonar, *Philosophy and Political Economy*, p. 72.

18 Windelband, *Die Geschichte der neueren Philosophie*, 1:154, 266, 276; Butler, *Sermons on Human Nature*, p. 93.

inclusive psychology of human drives, this new theory considered human behavior and especially the behavior termed moral to be at least in part initiated and formed by a person's inner reactions to the feelings of others.

The fully developed theory first appears as Hume's concept of "sympathy," but it can occasionally be glimpsed in earlier writings. Bacon, who otherwise assumed that the two main springs of human behavior were the drives toward individual and collective well-being, hinted at the importance of sympathetic imitation; he attempted to explain this phenomenon as a "transmission of spirits."[19] Hume's doctrine of sympathy was already implicit in Bishop Joseph Butler's theory, where moral feelings were seen as "reflection of affects." Butler "found that the motives for obeying moral laws, which he took as Divine commandments, were in part the reactions to anticipated judgments of our actions by God and man."[20] Even though Butler was the first to make the interaction of human minds an explanatory principle, he tended to apply it only as a practical rule to explain and validate a divine command already present in human nature.

For Hume, who denied the universal validity of the moral commandment, this doctrine of sympathy assumes the status of a fundamental principle, and his philosophy of ethics amounts to a sociology. Scottish ethical philosophy here throws off its normative trappings and appears simply as a descriptive and explanatory science.[21]

According to Hume, sympathy is a resonance between people's feelings, made possible by their identical constitution. Sympathy is brought about by one person's placing himself in the position of another and reproducing the other's feelings. Two factors are important: (1) this imitation of another person's feelings arises out of a certain natural necessity, and (2) the transmitted feelings

19 Jodl, *Geschichte der Ethik*, p. 198; Bacon, *De Aug. Scient.*, lib. IV, cap. 1, and *Sylva Sylvarum*, p. 112. Compare Dugald Stewart, vol. 3, who cited this passage from Bacon.

20 Windelband, *Geschichte der neueren Philosophie*, 1:276; Butler, *Sermons on Human Nature*, p. 42, 44.

21 Windelband, *Geschichte der neueren Philosophie*, 1:349.

produce corresponding reactions in the recipient, so that he reacts to the transmitted feelings exactly as if they had originated in himself.[22]

Hume's ethical doctrine was further developed by his friend and student Adam Smith in *The Moral Sentiment*, although no important changes were made in the basic principles. From Adam Smith the doctrine of sympathy reached modern social science by two separate paths. Dugald Stewart, one of Smith's followers, developed the psychological aspect of the theory and related it to the

22 Hume, *Human Nature*, 2:335. "We may begin with considering anew the nature and the force of sympathy. The minds of all men are similar in their feelings and operations; nor can any one be actuated by any affection of which all others are not in some degree susceptible. As strings equally wound up, the motion of one communicates itself to the rest; so all the affections readily pass from one person to another, and beget corresponding movements in every creature. When I see the effects of passion in the voice and gesture of any person, my mind immediately passes from the effect to their causes, and forms such a lively idea of the passion, as is presently converted into the passion itself."

Ibid., p. 350. "This principle of sympathy is of so powerful and insinuating a nature, that it enters into most of our sentiments and passions, and often takes *place under the appearance of its contrary.* For 'tis remarkable, that when a person opposes me in anything, which I am strongly bent upon, and rouses up my passion by contradiction, I have always a degree of sympathy for him, nor does my commotion proceed from any other origin. We may observe an evident conflict or recounter of principles and passions. On the one side there is that passion or sentiment, which is natural to me; and 'tis observable, that the stronger this passion is, the greater is the commotion. There must also be some passion or sentiment on the other side; and this passion can proceed from nothing but sympathy. The sentiments of others can never affect us, but by becoming, in some measure, our own; in which case they operate upon us, by opposing or increasing our passions, in the very same manner, as if they had been originally deriv'd from our own temper and disposition. While they remain concealed in the minds of others, they can never have any influence upon us: And even when they are known, if they went no further than the imagination, or conception; that faculty is so accustomed to objects of every kind, that a mere idea, tho' contrary to our sentiments and inclinations wou'd never alone be able to affect us."

Dugald Stewart, 3:116; Höffding, *Ethik*, pp. 39, 57, 229; Giddings, *Principles of Sociology*, pref. to 3d ed., p. 11. Compare also Guyau, *L'Irréligion de l'avenir*, pp. 341, 346.

phenomena of involuntary imitation and hypnotism. The sociological application of the principle is encountered in such varied works as Giddings's *Principles of Sociology*, and Höffding's ethical writings. In both cases the concept of sympathy is essentially applied as an explanatory principle, although Höffding does not interpret sympathy as formally as Giddings whose "consciousness of kind" is a transformation of Smith's principle.

This principle originally introduced by Hume and Smith can be recognized in still other forms in modern social psychology. Even the theory of those writers who view imitation as the specific form of sociological reaction can be viewed as an adoption of Hume's principle of sympathy, although there may be no basis for assuming a historical connection between both doctrines.[23] According to its name, the theory of imitation would explain only the transmission of an arbitrary movement or way of behaving from one person to another. In reality, however, the exponents of this doctrine interpret imitation approximately as Hume did, namely, the transmission of a feeling or an idea from one person to another. The second person is placed in the psychic situation of the first, and he reacts to the merely imagined stimulus which the first person actually experienced, in exactly the same way as if he had received the stimulus himself.[24]

Hume's and Smith's use of sympathy cannot be equated with the concept later encountered mainly in Spencer and Höffding, which identifies sympathetic reaction with deep rooted instincts such as maternal love, etc.[25] This "impulsive altruism," as Baldwin calls it, should not be confused with imitation in the sense in which Tarde and Baldwin use the term, nor with Hume's meaning of sympathy. For Hume, sympathy is a formal concept with much greater significance; it is intended to explain how people under-

23 Baldwin, *Social and Ethical Interpretations*, Foreword to 2d ed., p. 12; Tarde *Les Lois de l'imitation*, p. 85, and *Études de psychologie sociale*, p. 51; Bagehot, *Der Ursprung der Nationen*, p. 106.

24 Hume, *Human Nature*, 2:111; Smith, *Moral Sentiments*, p. 4; Tarde, *Les Lois de l'imitation*, Preface, p. 7.

25 Höffding, *Psychologie*, p. 305, and *Ethik*, p. 608; Spencer, *Psychology*, 2:558.

stand the feelings and inner life of their fellow men. It implies approximately what Jodl termed "the ability to reproduce the feelings of others."[26] The difference between Hume and the preceding writers lies precisely in the fact that for Hume sympathy is no longer exclusively a feeling such as pity, goodwill, etc., but a process through which these and other morally positive feelings and dispositions come into being.

The difference between sympathy and imitation[27] seems to lie less in the different nature of two processes, than in an emphasis on

26 Jodl, *Psychologie*, 2:329. "If the ability to reproduce the feelings of others in general is called 'fellow-feeling,' then it must be said that the development of feelings toward individuals is based, for the most part, on fellow-feeling. It is necessary to keep in mind that in this sense, fellow-feeling enters as an element both in one's own feelings and in the feelings of others. Accordingly, it is a much broader concept than feelings toward others of compassion or shared happiness, which are exclusively understood under the term fellow-feeling in common usage and unfortunately also in most scientific practice. For fellow-feeling, in the sense used here, occurs not only if the sorrows and joys of another are felt to be one's own; upon fellow-feeling rests the thankfulness and love under which we transform the benevolent attitude of another person into our own likings; upon it rest the enjoyment of another's misfortunes and the cruelty with which we feel another's pain not as our suffering but as his, and take satisfaction from our rejection and our evil-wishing. Fellow-feeling is the basis of the pride and shame, in which we duplicate or measure against our self-love, either the wonderment, respect, and honor or the ridicule, aversion, and contempt which others feel toward us or our accomplishments. And in the same sense of the above—that all feelings for others are based upon the experience of one's own feelings—the opposite must be said, namely, that all self-awareness receives its nourishment from the duplication of others' feelings, and would languish without it. On this basis, it seems advisable to completely reject the easily misunderstood term 'fellow-feeling' and instead of it to use the expression 'sympathy.' This term was introduced by English psychology in the past century for the phenomena of duplication of feelings which are under consideration here. The use of 'sympathy' by Hume and Smith, which was responsible for the first penetrating and until today basic research on related phenomena, is identical with what is understood here as 'fellow-feeling' in the most general sense."

Also see Hume, *Human Nature*, 2:112, 335, 350.

27 Tarde, *Études de Psychologie Sociale*, p. 291.

different sides of one and the same process. The common method of explaining this process today tends to view its psychological or conscious aspect as a by-product of the physiological aspect. This is in contrast to Hume. Rooted in the rationalistic psychology of his times, he viewed the idea as the origin, so that the entire process assumes a psychological—and in a certain sense, logical—character.[28] Whether this process is called sympathy, in accordance with Hume, or imitation, as with Tarde, what is essential is the emphasis placed on the formal aspect of the matter: the object of concern is a process, and not a feeling with a given content. In addition, there is no attempt to explain the origin of social feelings and drives. Instead, human drives as they have developed in history are taken for granted; and an attempt is then made to show how these drives interact and are transmitted.

III

Imitation as a process of communication is often discussed in modern psychological research, but up to now no clear concept of the process has emerged. What imitation actually is, remains unclear.[29] Without making a special study of imitation as a psychological process, however, it is possible to indicate both the diversity of social functions performed by imitation and the variety of forms it assumes in different social groups.[30]

28 Compare C. Lange, *Ueber Gemütsbewegungen*, [n. p.]; James, *Principles of Psychology*, 2:442.

29 See Baldwin, *Dictionary of Philosophy and Psychology*, where the various meanings of imitation, according to different authors, are presented and explained. Compare as well the writings of Tarde, Baldwin, and others, who have already been mentioned. Also see Epinas, *Des Sociétés animales*, pp. 358ff.; Royce, "The External World and Social Consciousness," *Philosophical Review*, 3 (September 1894): 513–45; Durkheim, *Le Suicide*, chap. 4; Bosanquet, *Mind*, April, 1898; Dewey, *Philosophical Review*, July 1898; Lloyd Morgan, *Animal Behaviour*, chap. 5; Wallace, *Natural Selection*, chap. 6; Groos, *Das Spiel der Menschen*, pt. 2, chap. 3; Giddings, *Inductive Sociology*, p. 105, and *The Principles of Sociology*, [n. p.]; Preyer, *Die Seele des Kindes*, pt. 2, chap. 12.

30 Royce provided a simple and clear explanation for the sociological importance of imitation in his article, "Selfconsciousness, Socialconscious-

To begin with, observation of the more highly developed animals shows that imitation is an important means of further developing and forming the dispositions that are inherited, namely, the instincts.[31] Here, imitation appears as an instinct-like behavior or even a reflex, as for example in the frequently observed contagion of yawning. This can only be explained by positing the presence of a disposition for yawning; seeing the action merely provides the precipitating stimulus which releases the imitative movement. The readiness of the psycho-physical organism for the suggestion is characteristic for this primary form of imitation. Animals only imitate those actions that inheritance has prepared them for.[32]

---

ness, and Nature." See *Studies of Good and Evil*, p. 219. "From infancy on, my fellow's expressive acts get a meaning to me as the suggestion of his concrete inner life, just in so far as I am able to imitate these deeds of his by bodily acts of my own, brought to pass under conditions like those in which he, my fellow, acts. For when I definitely repeat a bodily act that expresses any human meaning, the act, as I repeat it, under definite conditions, gets for me an inner meaning, which I could never grasp so long as I merely observed such an act from without, as an event in my perceived phenomenal world. But this inner meaning which the act gets when I repeat it, becomes for me the objective meaning of the act as my fellow performs it; and thus the meaning of the imitated act, interpreted for me at the moment of my imitation, gets conceived as the real meaning, the inner experience of my fellow, at the moment when he performs the act which is my model. If you laugh I know what you mean just in so far as, under similar conditions, I can join with you and laugh heartily also, and can thus, by fully imitating your deed, get a sense of your meaning. But if I see you laughing under circumstances that absolutely forbid me even to conceive myself as imitating your expression of mirth, then I have frankly to say that I do not in the least know what you mean by laughing at just this situation, and so cannot conceive in so far what your inner experience is."

31 Romanes, *Geistige Entwicklung in Tierreich*, pp. 238ff.

32 Lloyd Morgan, *Animal Behaviour*, p. 189. "It is probable that in animals imitation has its foundations in instinctive behaviour, of which it may be regarded as the characteristically social type. If one of a group of chicks learns by casual experience to drink from a tin of water, others will run up and peck at the water and thus learn to drink. A hen teaches her little ones to pick up grain or other food by pecking on the ground, and dropping suitable materials before them, while they seemingly imitate her by picking up the grain."

Behavior which is transferred by imitation from one generation to another is called tradition. Here, tradition is opposed to instinct which is received only through inheritance. Whenever animal tradition is discussed, it refers to behavior received through transmission, such as singing and nest construction by birds, which is not inherited but must be learned through imitation.[33]

A similar effect of imitation is seen in humans. People learn speech and other habits and social customs by means of half-conscious or reflex suggestion.[34] The amount of behavior learned in this way is much greater in humans; that is, animal tradition is very limited. On the other hand there are relatively more instincts in animals than in humans.[35]

It would be a mistake, however, to suppose that the entire sociological significance of imitation lies in the transfer of tradition from one generation to another. It is necessary to consider the great number of reflex and sensorimotor suggestions through which members of a group affect each other at every moment.[36]

33 Ibid., pp. 220ff.

34 Ibid., pp. 221ff. "In the first place, it is probable that, as in other modes of animal behaviour, traditional procedure is founded on an instinctive basis. This must be an imitative tendency of the broad follow-my-leader type. . . . Where this instinctive tendency is only partly or incompletely specialized along certain lines of behaviour, we should have at this stage certain hereditary trends of action, dependent on stimuli afforded by the behaviour of others."

35 Ibid., p. 176. "We may term this reserve fund of intelligent accommodation, this inherited ability to meet specially difficult circumstances as they arise, *innate capacity*. From the nature of the case it must be indefinite, for it must carry with it the ability to meet unforeseen combinations of the environing forces by new combinations of the results of experience. Its distinguishing mark is plasticity, in contradistinction to the stereotyped fixity of typical instinct. And accompanying its evolution there is probably, as we have seen, a dissolution of its antithesis,—instinct. Thus may we account for the fact that man, with his great store of innate capacity, has so small a number of stereotyped instincts."

36 C. Lange, *Sinnengenüsse und Kunstgenuss*, p. 43. "It must be clearly understood that the interpretation through eye and ear of physical expression of an emotion is capable of immediately calling forth—without any intervening psychic link—the same phenomena that are being observed in another. Seen from the physiological standpoint, the matter is

As a result, repeated suggestion serves to increasingly reinforce usage and behavior once it is learned, and in addition, individuals are continually under a kind of psychic constraint which can be viewed as the sum or the result of all this mutual suggestion. Through continual practice, social usage takes on the form of individual habit; it becomes firmly established in the psycho-physical organism.[37] Once established, these habits are practiced with a feeling of obligation which reacts with indignation to any transgression by others. An important product of the sociological process is thus revealed in the way that the group as a whole exerts coercion upon the individual.[38]

The various forms of interaction resulting in such direct control of the individual by the whole were included by Spencer under the term "ceremonial control." He saw this as the most primitive and the most general form of social control.[39] All ele-

---

very remarkable, or in other words, very obscure. At the same time, it is not an isolated phenomenon; instead, it presents a single expression of a comprehensive psycho-physiological phenomenon of great importance: This is the unconscious, instinctive impulse which every person has to immediately imitate for himself a movement or a sound which he hears by another; this occurs by means of the imitation of muscular movement, as in every other sympathetic imitation. Actually, this imitative drive does not play an extremely large role in people's lives—people do not continually run after one another in order to imitate because there is simultaneously a desire to control and suppress this drive. It is also inhibited by circumstances; the imitative drive makes itself felt especially when very pronounced phenomena are present and are attentively observed."

Baldwin, *Mental Development*, chap. 6, differentiates between physiological (reflex), sensorimotor, and ideomotor suggestion. The sympathetic imitation which Lange speaks about here, is a kind of sensorimotor suggestion.

37 Wundt, in *Ethik*, 1:108–28, has clearly differentiated between habits, mores, and general usages.

38 Durkheim, *Revue Philosophique*, May 1894, pp. 466ff.; Ross, *Social Control*, p. 146.

39 Spencer, *The Principles of Sociology*, 2:5. "That ceremonial restraint, preceding other forms of restraint, continues ever to be the most widely-diffused form of restraint, we are shown by such facts as that in all intercourse between members of each society, the decisively governmental actions are usually prefaced by this government of observances. The em-

mentary forms of social restrictions are thus expressed as social habits which are upheld through the reflex-suggestive interaction of individuals within a group. All subsequent forms of control are based upon these.

If animal and human societies are compared, fundamental differences appear and must be considered. When animals come into the world they possess a set of instincts which completely define both their dispositions and the behavior based on them. As a result, the amount of new behavior which animals can acquire is limited by the degree to which its instinct-like form is present in their inherited dispositions.[40] Furthermore, the dispositions themselves, which are not yet defined at birth, become fixed into habits soon afterward. Thus in animals every impulse appears to lead immediately to a predetermined action, and to one which is predetermined in the same way for every other member of the same species. Animals exhibit relatively little individuality. Objects which might catch their attention always have one and the same meaning for all individuals of the same species. It is otherwise with humans whose instinctive actions are relatively few and whose acquired behavior is relatively predominant. It follows that humans, unlike animals, have to first learn through experience how to react to various stimuli. Furthermore, precisely because the experience of every individual differs from that of his fellow men, the meaning of the outside world is different for every individual.

---

bassy may fail, negotiation may be brought to a close by war, coercion of one society by another may set up wider political rule with its peremptory commands; but there is habitually this more general and vague regulation of conduct preceding the more special and definite. So within a community, acts of relatively stringent control coming from ruling agencies, civil and religious, begin with and are qualified by this ceremonial control; which not only initiates but in a sense envelopes all other. . . . Modified forms of action caused in men by the presence of their fellows, constitute that comparatively vague control out of which other more definite controls are evolved—the primitive undifferentiated kind of government from which the political and religious governments are differentiated, and in which they ever continue immersed."

40 Wundt, *Ethik*, 1:107ff.

Related to this is the fact that human actions are not always dictated by immediate motives, but to some degree by ideal ones. The explanation of this begins with the human capacity to conceptualize ideas. The world becomes infinitely more complicated as soon as what is can be compared to what was. In addition, humans possess the ability to communicate their thoughts and feelings to a much higher degree than do animals, and as a result the world in which men live sustains a variety of meanings which the world of animals cannot have. Through interaction, men's dispositions are continually altered, and their total being thereby gains a certain plasticity. The more flexible individuals are, and the greater the number of deliberate as well as unconscious actions that they are capable of, the more diverse will be the meanings of the objects to which these actions are directed.[41]

If man seems to have partially lost the quality of immediacy, it only means that he does not react to every stimulus and does not obey every impulse as if it embodied the world's total meaning in that moment. Instead, men tend to view every experience as the result of a previous one, and as the indication of one to follow. The full meaning of a conceived object does not lie in the impulse which it immediately stimulates; instead, the object takes on significance only when it is understood in its relationships, and when the first response is modified by those impulses associated with it. In this way, the world of men acquires a double meaning, one immediate and the other indirect. This double meaning of objects, under which every other object not only has immediate and individual significance, but is seen as a sign and symbol for other objects and other meanings, occurs only in the world of men and differentiates it from the world of animals.

Precisely because men do not surrender unconditionally to every impulse but generally direct their actions according to ideal motives, there arises from the world of perceptions, which is differ-

41 Münsterberg, *Grundzüge*, p. 551. "To comprehend an object means that we take on a special method of behaving. . . . the particular kind of motor attitude is the basis for the special kind of comprehension. Thus the meaning of a word can be comprehended uniquely as a motor attitude."

ent for every individual, a world of ideas which is identical for all. This separation is not found in animal consciousness. Animals act only within a world of perceptions.[42] Each object's meaning is established at the moment of its perception, instead of being assigned only when the object has assumed its position in an ideal order. In animals, perception is immediately followed by its corresponding action. Thus interaction among animals appears as a direct transference of one individual's action to another. In a herd, only those actions are imitated which have the character of a reflex, such as the expression of feelings, a cry of danger, etc. The imitating movement will have the same character as the one imitated. The entire sociological process presumes that members of the herd possess totally conforming and complementary dispositions which are activated by the mutually suggestive effect of similar movements.[43]

A similar kind of reciprocal interaction does exist among men. In this direct manner, each generation has taken on a large part of its traditions from the preceding generation. Language, usages, and the whole ceremonial aspect of daily social life are learned through an only partially conscious imitation. Men possess an inherited predisposition for speech as well as for other social functions, and the cultivation of these functions takes place through natural imitation of surrounding social forms. Because men are not totally engaged in their individual acts, but continue thinking, and because they view ongoing action as a means of attaining a preconceived goal, they are not subject to the domination of this process of reciprocity in the same sense that animals

42 Calderwood, *Evolution and Man's Place in Nature*, p. 124. "Sensitiveness in the organism, succession of sensory impressions in the history of the life, and correlation of these with activity through the nerve centers, are characteristics of all organic life, including that of the insect with that of the man. What, then, is it which is peculiar to man? It is his rational discrimination in advance of sensory discrimination. All organisms feel contact and act in response to it. All human life not only does these two things, but also interprets experience, thereby forming a knowledge of the things with which the sensitive organism comes into contact."

Compare Romanes, *The Psychic Development of Men*, pp. 21ff.

43 Lloyd Morgan, *Animal Behaviour*, chap. 5.

are. Men can submit to the coercion exerted by the whole on the individual and subject themselves to group customs while still allowing completely individual motives to determine their behavior. The individual can even make use of the existence of usages and social behavior as a means to obtain his personal end. This actually occurs in everyday life wherever social organization serves to further individual goals. The economic organization of society presents a social pattern in which every other individual within the totality appears only as a means for the attainment of an individual's happiness. It is precisely from this perspective that classical political economy has interpreted society.

As Simmel has already noted, barter is "an unique sociological institution, an original form and function of social interaction"; it can be added that this only occurs among humans.[44] Barter exhibits a secondary form of reciprocity that can be included under the concept of imitation. In this case, a person employs the psychophysical mechanism of speech to project himself into the mental situation of the other, while acting in the opposite manner. The example of the barter relationship will be discussed later; it is necessary to point out here that the primitive form of reciprocity observed in the animal herd is also continually active in human groups. Among humans reciprocity forces all individuals to accept a uniformity in the formal aspects of social life, expressed in usage and fashion. This uniformity is purely formal and external; its importance dwindles the further the social forms are from the "natural" forms of animal society. Thus in social life, in culture, it is seen that suggestive imitation—the primary form of reciprocity—only determines the style of life, but not life itself.

IV

In general, the concept of "primary reciprocity" used above coincides with what Tarde understood as "imitation." For him imitation was nothing more than a special kind of "universal repetition," special in that it enables behavior initiated by outstanding individuals to spread throughout society and to become

44 Simmel, *Philosophie des Geldes*, p. 56.

common to all. "Social" would thus be defined as what is initiated and diffused throughout society in this manner.[45] Thus Tarde viewed social life as trivial and meaningless compared to the life of the individuals active within it; for whatever was repeated by masses of people in this mechanical way could only be superficial and meaningless.

Baldwin's concept of imitation is essentially different from Tarde's. For Baldwin, the importance of imitation was not that the same action is repeated by all members of a group, nor that this behavior is diffused among a number of individuals. Instead, imitation is important as a process enabling individuals to affect the inner life of each other. Out of this reciprocity, personalities are developed.[46] The value of imitation as a social function lies not in the external, formal side of repeated behavior but rather in the repercussions of the repeated action in the personality of individuals. In other words, imitation is important because it induces new dispositions in individuals.[47] Baldwin viewed the process of imitation solely from the side of the individual and in so doing discovered the special problem which differentiates social psychology from sociology. The same process of imitation must now be viewed from the side of the group, from the sociological side.[48]

In certain social groupings, such as parliament or a court of law, a kind of reciprocity occurs whose function is not only to carry out collective action, but free from external considerations, to direct the collective action toward changing the disposition of

45 Tarde, *Les Lois de l'imitation*, p. 76. "A society is always, in different degrees, an association; and an association is to sociability, to imitation, what organization is to life, or even what molecular composition is to the elasticity of space. . . . Proceeding from there, if we wish to keep the analogy in the three realms, it is necessary to see that life is simply the organized sensitivity of protoplasm, that matter is simply the organized elasticity of space, just as society is only organized imitation."

Compare Tarde, *Psychologie économique*, 1:7ff.; and Baldwin, *Social and Ethical Interpretations*, p. 496.

46 Baldwin, *Social and Ethical Interpretations*, pt. 1, chap. 1, "The Imitative Person."

47 Ibid., pp. 539ff.

48 Ibid., p. 531; Tosti, "Social Psychology and Sociology," *Psychological Review*, July, 1898, p. 547.

the group itself or of some of its members. This kind of institution thus presents examples of formal processes in which a collectivity acts upon itself.

The processes through which the social group defines itself differ essentially from those found in animal herds; they are also different from Tarde's imitative processes. As a sociological activity, Tarde's imitative process can be compared to the association process in psychology, where dispositions already acquired by the group appear to guide the course of action between individuals. However, the process discussed above tends to be more like the processes of attention or perception. The examples of parliament and court can be viewed as only an adjustment and adaptation by the group as a whole to a situation; thus it is not a matter of an action in the normal sense of the word, but rather only of the preliminaries of an action.

The sociological processes seen operating in parliament or courts are characteristic of similar processes which can be observed in other groups, but the former are much more complicated and therefore more difficult to analyze. The simplest form of this process can be best observed in the crowd. Again, the term "crowd" has the same meaning here as in collective psychology; it cannot be equated to the wandering hordes that are similar to animal herds nor to masses seized by panic, the closest human approximation to herds of animals.[49]

The crowd must be viewed more as the result of a specific sociological process whose general characteristics are those which generate collective attention. If a large number of individuals stop on a busy street to watch a passing parade or to listen to a street-corner speaker, this is an example of collective attention. Still more striking examples of the same sociological process can be

49 Panic is a social form which has not yet been handled by the school of collective psychology. A description of it is found in Max Wirth, *Geschichte der Handelskrisen*. Compare also Sidis, *Psychology of Suggestion*, pp. 343ff.; and Stoll, *Suggestion und Hypnotismus*, pp. 450ff. There is a continually recurring tendency among different writers to view the crowd as a historical concept rather than as a purely scientific one, applicable in any age. See Sighele, *Psychologie des Sectes*, p. 37; Tarde, *Philosophie pénale*, [n. p.]; and Sidis, *Psychology of Suggestion*, p. 310.

seen in the effects of modern advertising whose entire technology consists of controlling the mechanism for directing attention. This very example clearly illustrates a sociological process which cannot be seen simply as the sum of individual psychological processes: the desired effect results more from interaction between people than from direct suggestion.

A more or less well-defined kind of collective focus is always present when people are together. In the larger realm of politics and in the small world of intimate social life, certain general concerns that dominate thoughts and conversation are always present. Today it is the Asian war, last year it was England and the Boers; and still earlier it was the Dreyfus affair which captured the attention of the whole world.

Thus collective attention appears as a process in which the group acts upon itself; that is, the group takes a stand on something in its environment. Here, collective attention is directly the opposite of the process described earlier which enabled social usages to establish and perpetuate themselves in society. For through collective attention, customs and the more stable forms of social interaction are loosened and finally dissolved. This can best be seen in the crowd where collective attention takes on a more intense expression than usual. Wherever crowd consciousness develops, whether in a gathering of people who collect in the street, or in a whole nation, the usual course of social life is interrupted and normal social activity is disturbed. In times of great ferment, not only limits set by laws but also those of tradition and custom fall away.[50]

50 Friedmann, *Wahnideen im Völkerleben*, p. 259; Le Bon, *Psychologie du socialisme*, p. 93; Lombroso, *Die Anarchisten*, p. 21; Förstemann, *Die christliche Geisslergesellschaft*, p. 43. Stoll, in *Suggestion und Hypnotismus*, [n. p.], reports the effect of the Crusades as follows: "The idea of the Crusades absorbed all other interests; in the enthusiasm for it, the struggles of politics were silenced, and even the bonds of family life were lightly offered up to it. Inhabitants of cloisters left their quiet shelter, hermits their woods and wildernesses, in order to enter the ranks of the Crusaders. Even thieves and robbers left their haunts in order to confess their deeds and, as penance, to take on the cross and turn to the Holy Land. Merchants and handworkers left their livelihoods; what could not

The first result of this heightened attention is a restriction of normal impulses and normal associations, which is the same as increased suggestibility. This heightened suggestibility is precisely the characteristic trait of the crowd. Sidis pointed out two stages in the development of crowd consciousness. In the first stage, group suggestibility is heightened through "indirect" suggestion. Suggestibility increases continually until it finally reaches a condition approximating hypnosis. This is the second stage; the crowd now reacts to "direct" suggestion, often with the impulsiveness of someone who is hypnotized. In this stage the crowd appears as the plastic instrument of its leader whose suggestion is followed without any resistance. At this point the crowd changes into a popular riot.[51]

Precisely because the crowd proves to be a social power whose effect is always more or less disruptive and revolutionary, it seldom arises where there is social stability and where customs have deep roots. In contrast, where social bonds are removed and old institutions weakened, great crowd movements develop more easily and forcefully. From a sociological standpoint, this explains, at least in part, the significance of the strike. This is a movement whose first goal is to draw the public's attention to a condition considered unjust and unbearable by the workers. It is an appeal to the judgment of the whole because no existing court has jurisdiction. This means of appealing to the public results in the interruption of normal activity for large numbers of people. Thus it

---

be taken on the journey lost its value and was sold at low prices to those remaining behind. The price of food declined so much that surpluses existed in the middle of famine. Miracles and various kinds of heavenly signs intensified the general madness. . . . People who had originally mocked the excited bustle of the Crusades were gradually affected by the general activity—a characteristic of the imitative effect of suggestion. Regretting their earlier indifference, they replaced it with a zeal which was no less intense than the ecstacy of those at whom they had once laughed. The general ferment engaged everyone's mind in such a manner that even in those times of political and public insecurity, common theft, burglary, and arson ceased without any effort on the part of the government."

51 Sidis, *Psychology of Suggestion*, pp. 18ff., 297ff.

provides the conditions for a crowd movement and eventually for a popular riot.

It is seen that the great crowd movements of the Middle Ages, the Crusades, and the smaller movements which preceded and accompanied the Reformation arose at a time when social ties were weakened and a feeling of common identity had disappeared from society.[52] But it was through these very crowd movements that a new collective spirit developed. The Renaissance followed the Crusades, and out of the ruins of the Church new sects arose.[53] Crowd movements played a double role here—they were the forces which dealt the final blow to old existing institutions, and they introduced the spirit of the new ones. According to Le Bon's formulation of this dual role, the crowd is a phenomenon seen at the beginning and at the end of a cultural development.[54]

A closer study of collective attention shows that it must generally be considered an inhibiting process. Within the boundaries of a social group, personalities produce a restricting effect on each other. Le Bon as well as Sighele noted that with the development of the crowd consciousness, the motor impulses characteristic of the individual are suppressed. At the same time, the motor impulses common to all individuals are heightened.[55] This phenomenon is explained in the following manner. It is now known that emotions are very contagious, especially in gatherings of people, for example in a political meeting. Under such conditions the emotional excitement of each individual penetrates the entire group; this is accomplished through the process of unconscious imitation. Where everyone's attention is directed to the same object, there

52 Hecker, *Der schwarze Tod*, p. 42; Schmidt, *Histoire de la secte des Cathares ou Albigeois*, 1:59, 142; Lippert, *Christentum, Volksglaube und Volksbrauch*, p. 574; Förstemann, *Die christliche Geisslergesellschaft*, p. 19; Symonds, *Renaissance in Italy*, vol. 1, "The Age of the Despots," chap. 7 and app. 4; Taine, *L'Ancien régime*, bk. 5, chap. 9-2.

53 Adler, *Geschichte des Sozialismus und Kommunismus*, pt. 1, bk. 3, "Kommunismus und Anarchismus als Konsequenzen christlich-reformatorischer Tendenzen." See especially chap. 2, pp. 91ff.

54 Le Bon, *Psychologie des foules*, p. 188.

55 Ibid., p. 17; Sighele, *Psychologie des Auflaufs*, pp. 12ff.

appears a kind of reciprocity which takes the form of a circular movement. Baldwin understood imitation primarily as a circular process: once an organism receives a stimulus, it attempts to place itself so that it receives the same stimulus again.[56] The simplest form of this circular process occurs in the heliotropism of plants which show a disposition to turn in the direction from which they receive either a pleasant or a life-giving stimulus.[57] In higher forms this circular process is expressed as a process of directing attention.[58]

Such a circular process occurs, in the sociological sense, when two individuals imitate each other reciprocally. This can take the simple form of A imitating B, and B imitating A. As long as emotions are involved which can be imitated in this manner, B receives from A a reflection of his own feelings. Thus both are involved in a circular process where each one, in imitating the other, increases his own emotional stimulation. The same process is seen in a more complicated form where A imitates B, B imitates C, and C again imitates A.

If this entire process is understood as an inhibiting process, the inhibition occurring through the first imitation is heightened by each following one. This continues as long as everybody's attention is directed to the same object, because every motion of A, B, and C results in the individual's receiving more of the same stimulus. The inhibitions accompanying each successive imitation introduce a condition of suggestibility in the group. Suggestibility, however, is identical to attention and can therefore be called a process of collective attention.[59]

56 Baldwin, *Mental Development in the Child and the Race*, p. 133. "The essential thing then, in imitation, over and above a simple ideo-motor suggestion, is that the stimulus starts a motorprocess which tends to reproduce the stimulus and through it the motorprocess again. From the physiological side we have a circular activity—sensor, motor; sensor, motor; and from the psychological side we have a similar circle—reality, image, movement; reality, image, movement, etc."

57 Ibid., p. 180.

58 Stout, *A Manual of Psychology*, p. 271.

59 Münsterberg, *Grundzüge*, p. 550.

V

From the above it is now clear that the development of a crowd involves a process by which individuals unconsciously and without any premeditation join together as a unit. The unity of the crowd is based on the fact that all members of the group are controlled by one common drive evoked by the reciprocal interaction of these members. This reciprocity works as an inhibiting process suppressing all purely individual impulses, so that the only associations remaining in the individual's consciousness are those which merge with the ideas shaped by the reciprocal process. If it is characteristic of the crowd that all its members are controlled by a common drive and that all purely individual impulses and interests are inhibited, then it is characteristic of the public that individual impulses and interests arise out of the undefined basis of the common consciousness and develop further in a peculiar reciprocal interaction.

Before the concept of public is examined more closely, the process of reciprocity between those interests arising within the public must be clearly understood. Within the social totality these reciprocal interests are represented by parties, such as political parties, schools, sects, etc., which check and define each other. Just as politics always presents a liberal and a conservative party in opposition to one another, so in economic activities—where the individualization of interests is more pronounced—the buyer and seller are involved in the same reciprocal relationship. In each case, the one side presumes the existence of the opposite one, and neither of the two could be exactly what it is without the other.[60] In sects, the role of this opposition as a force in group formation is less apparent. It cannot be directly stated that the existence of one sect is dependent upon the existence of another. To be sure,

60 Bluntschli, *Charakter und Geist der politischen Parteien*, p. 3. "Parties are the physically necessary appearance and expression of their inner drives which motivate the political life of the nation. The party is, as the word 'pars' indicates, only a part of a larger whole, never this totality itself. . . . No party can stand alone by itself; only the opposite party makes possible its existence and its development."

it is only through its opposition to other sects or even to the world at large, that a sect gains consciousness of its unique position in the totality. Its unique significance and character are soon altered when this opposition no longer exists. In general it is the same with groups as with individuals: they attain self-consciousness only by opposing other groups. The concepts they form of themselves are always interlaced with images of other groups.[61]

This special reciprocal relationship into which groups as well as individuals fall, has been studied from several fundamental viewpoints. Tarde devoted an entire essay to defining the concept, and he attempted to reduce this kind of social interaction to one form of a general process, *contre-répétition*. Opposition, he stated, is merely a special kind of imitation.[62] Baldwin and Royce, in contrast, viewed imitation and opposition—in other words the drive for self-assertion—as parallel processes active whenever people join together.[63] The reciprocity of these two processes (the particularizing and the generalizing processes) was used by Baldwin in attempting to explain not only the development of the self-

61 Royce, *Studies of Good and Evil*, chap. 7, "Anomalies of Self-Consciousness," p. 196. "Selfconscious functions are all of them, in their finite, human and primary aspect, social functions, due to the habits of human intercourse. They involve the presentation of some contrast between Ego and non-Ego."

62 Tarde, *L'Opposition universelle*, p. 10. "I mean, this tendency to think that one is original because one has contradicted common opinion or the common example. Here it is still a kind of imitation, and not less common in those pretentious circles where one is proud not to copy one's father, neighbor, or superior, even when he is better; but no, while negating precisely what the other affirms, while blaming that which he praises, while destroying precisely what he constructs, one convinces himself not to imitate the other person."

Compare also Tarde, *Les Lois de l'imitation*, Preface, 2d ed., p. 11. "There are, in effect, two means of imitation: to do exactly what his model does, or to do exactly the contrary."

63 Baldwin, in *Social and Ethical Interpretations*, p. 242, cites the following from a letter written by Royce: "I think there is here one very general factor neglected which deserves more study. One great region of social functioning consists in deliberately producing what I have called 'social contrast effects.' Questioning, criticism, social obstinacy, gossip

conscious individual, but also the development of social forms which bind these individuals into a unity.[64]

The process of social differentiation and the various forms assumed by social opposition are presented by Simmel in a series of very original works containing many meticulous and interesting observations.[65] He views social differentiation sociologically, that is, from the side of the collectivity, and thus differs from Royce and Baldwin, who approach it from the psychological or individual side.[66] In general, the same process is called "contra-imitation" by

---

about one's neighbor, opposition repartee, the social game of the sexes, in all its deliberate forms—these are functions, whose conscious purpose is not to reduce unity, not to decrease varieties, but to find, to bring out, and to dwell upon differences amongst selves. Such functions make up a fair half of social conscious life. They obscure imitative elements actually so universal, so that for most people, the discovery of the universality of imitation comes as a surprise, like the surprise of learning that one has always been talking prose.

"Well, as I notice, a great deal of an individual's inventiveness is a function due to the appearance of social contrast effects. Light up my conscious contents by some new contrast with the ideas of another, and I see, in myself, what I never saw before, and now I have 'a new idea.' One of the great, psychologically potent purposes of social life is the purpose to find oneself different from another self. The purpose is often vain, and its conscious expressions are full of illusions amusing to the on-looker, but of all grades of social organization, from the children in the market place to the nations stubbornly holding aloof from one another prating of glory and levying tariffs, one could assert with a force almost equal to that of Tarde's definition, that: society is a mutual display of mental contrasts."

64 Baldwin, *Social and Ethical Interpretations*, bk. 2, "Society," pp. 459ff.

65 Simmel, "Ueber soziale Differenzierung," *Schmollers Staats- und Sozialwissenschaftliche Forschungen*, vol. 10, 1890; Simmel, *Philosophie des Geldes*, chap. 4, "Die individuelle Freiheit," pp. 279ff.; Simmel, *American Journal of Sociology*, 9:4.

66 Baldwin, *Social and Ethical Interpretations*, p. 531. "In the study of social process, it is clear, we may take the point of view of social psychology—that of the question, by what mental process men actually are social and show social organization. But it is possible also to take the point of view of sociology—that of the question, what do I as an observer find going on between or among men who are socially organized."

Compare also C. Bouglé, *Les Idées égalitaires*.

Tarde, "opposition" by Baldwin and Royce, and "social differentiation" by Simmel.

For the purposes of more precisely characterizing and describing the sociological process called "opposition," it can be seen as a special form of competition. This is a concept taken from biology, while opposition, as defined by Baldwin and Royce, is in the first instance a psychological term. If opposition is viewed from the side of the individual, its connection with the term competition is immediately obvious. What appears as a drive for self-assertion in the individual consciousness is seen from the side of the collectivity, where these drives are in conflict, as a special form of the universal struggle for existence.

What differentiates the sociological from the biological process is the realms in which they operate. Biological opposition takes place in the physical realm, where the opposed interests are physical forces which mutually limit each other, as for example, when one species kills off another or drives it from the area in which it lives. The sociological process of opposition takes place instead within the consciousness of the individuals involved; it appears as a process of individual interests and ideals shaping and adapting to each other.[67]

War, a crude form of social competition, has as its goal not so much the annihilation as the suppression of the opponent. It is not only the drive for material gain, but also the drive for domination that causes a nation to test its power in war against other nations. It is often clear enough that the drive for self-assertion, which frequently leads to conflict between individuals as well as between nations, is satisfied as soon as one party's sense of honor or prestige is saved and made secure by defeat and humiliation of the opponent. The victor does not demand the destruction of his opponent but is satisfied with the symbolic recognition of his own superiority and dominance—in addition to other more material settlements. A similar observation can be made when two hostile armies

67 Fouilée, *La Psychologie des idées-forces*, 2:18. "Once formed, the image of others becomes a set idea, or rather, a collection of set ideas, always present in our consciousness, on which we always rely and which manifest their influence in all our actions, in all our movements."

prepare for battle; the mere presence and behavior of one side exerts a powerful influence on the other, demonstrating again that not only physical but psychological forces are involved.[68] Where the victory of one army over the other leads to a new constellation of psychological influences, this can be given a similar social-psychological explanation. Upon this rests the great importance of the symbols offered up by one side to indicate that it surrenders to the other; through the ceremony of handing over the sword, or whatever it may be, the change in the situation is recognized by both parties and proclaimed to all the world.[69] Psychologically, the events occurring in the consciousness of the victor and the vanquished are completely different, but seen sociologically, they are merely forces in a single process.

It is especially characteristic for the social-psychological process as here understood, that the events taking place in the mind of one member of the group are always allied to corresponding mental processes of other members. Only then can the varied individual psychological processes assume the status of a collective process, for actually, only those phenomena can be explained in a social-psychological sense which can be related to a collective consciousness.[70]

68 Ibid., vol. 1, Introduction.

69 Compare Spencer, *Sociology*, vol. 2, chap. 6, "Obeisances," where the various forms of submission are described, and where their development out of the primitive forms of emotional expression is presented.

70 Münsterberg, *Grundzüge*, p. 558. "The content of social consciousness is related to the social organism in the same way as the content of individual consciousness is to the single brain. In the collectivity, then, the individual brain enters as a social neuron whose protoplasmic processes exist in the system of sense organs, and whose route of discharge is represented by the entire external motor apparatus. Even the one-celled neurons of the individual brain are not fused, but are only placed next to each other so that one somehow influences the other. Precisely in this way, the social neurons influence each other, and out of the interaction of their alliances and oppositions, there develops the psychophysical life of the collectivity. . . . In special psychology, there is a procession from elements to ideas and attitudes, and out of their interaction the personality is formed. Thus, as psychology begins with the varieties of elements in the individual, the study of social psychology begins with the variety of personalities, and out of this, the forms of social life are systematically and synthetically represented as emerging from the interaction of personalities."

This becomes important when the characteristics of the public are again examined. The previously mentioned differences between crowd and public—namely, the inhibition of individual impulses and interests in the crowd, opposed to their emergence in the public—does not prevent understanding what takes place in the public as a collective process.[71] In fact, it appears merely as a modification of the imitation process already observed in the crowd, for social opposition assumes that opponents such as buyer and seller, conservative and liberal, etc., reciprocally imagine themselves in the position of the other, and that the feelings and behavior of one individual are directed and defined in his consciousness by imitating the feelings and behavior of the other individual.[72] All feelings which Jodl called human feelings take for granted the existence of social opposition, for only to the degree that people enter into opposition with others are they able to feel pride, pity, joy at another's misfortune, etc.[73]

71 [Ed. note: Footnote reference missing in text.] Ibid., p. 134. "Thus, within the boundaries of social psychology, it is again possible to differentiate between those processes, such as politics, science, art, law, religion, which presume individual behavior according to plan, and those such as language, myth, mores, which proceed from the drives of the crowd. The study of the latter can again be limited to the psychology of national types, but this differentiation is secondary."

72 Baldwin, *Social and Ethical Interpretations*, p. 15. "If it be true, as much evidence goes to show, that what the person thinks as himself is a pole or terminus at one end of an opposition in the sense of personality generally, and that the other pole or terminus is the thought he has of the other person, the 'alter,' then it is impossible to isolate his thought of himself at any time and say that in thinking of himself he is not essentially thinking of the alter also."

Baldwin, *Mental Development in the Child and the Race*, p. 335. "The 'Ego' and the 'alter' are thus born together. . . . My sense of myself grows by imitation of you and my sense of yourself grows in terms of my sense of myself. But 'Ego' and 'alter' are thus essentially social: each is a socius and each is an imitative creation."

73 Jodl, *Psychologie*, 2:386. "At this stage of primary awareness-development, the mind is only affected by immediate feelings, with which, as a result of previous experience, their cause is associated. At the stage of secondary awareness-development, thought processes replace and supplement the immediate impressions."

Compare Stout, *A Manual of Psychology*, pp. 580ff.

Social opposition is therefore a process which can be viewed from two perspectives. Approached psychologically, it appears as a process through which the individual attains self-awareness; from the sociological or social-psychological viewpoint, social opposition is a process of bringing individuals into reciprocal relationships with a more or less permanent, systematic character. An example of such reciprocity is seen in the relationship of ruler and subject, teacher and pupil, etc. These are all, to be sure, subjective determinations, but they have assumed a certain objective validity either by becoming established in tradition or by being generally recognized. Thus it can be said that the individual comes to know himself and finds his position within the collectivity through (1) imitation of his fellow men and (2) competition with them.[74]

Where social opposition has assumed a permanent and more or less systematic form, certain concurrent social psychological phenomena develop which are of special interest here. An example of such a phenomenon is the price of goods on the market. Buyer and seller have completely different interests in the goods; one wants to obtain them, the other to dispose of them. The price can be seen as the product resulting from the interaction of the two opposed interests; it is set neither by the subjective evaluation of buyer or seller, nor by the absolute or objective value of the object; instead the price is established by the reciprocal interaction of the different individual viewpoints and the opposing interests.

A similar product of social opposition is what is called prestige. Prestige originates in the recognition of a remarkable action. It is then attached by association to objects and individuals related only secondarily to the recognized deed, as when the prestige of the father passes to the son or even to other relatives bearing the same name. This demonstrates that what is in itself subjective becomes reified and then proceeds to function as a natural power in society. This is best seen in the phenomena of social epidemics.[75]

Public opinion is a social-psychological phenomenon which

74 Cooley, "Personal Competition," *Economic Studies* 4 (April 2, 1899): 78, 149.

75 Compare Spencer, *Sociology*, vol. 1, chap. 20, p. 280, where Spencer presents the development of ancestor worship.

results from the critical behavior of various opposed individuals or groups. However, what is usually called a public is a kind of group which stands for the most part at the same stage of awareness-development as the crowd. Thus, so-called public opinion is generally nothing more than a naive collective impulse which can be manipulated by catchwords. Modern journalism, which is supposed to instruct and direct public opinion by reporting and discussing events, usually turns out to be simply a mechanism for controlling collective attention. The "opinion" formed in this manner shows a form that is logically similar to the judgment derived from unreflective perception: the opinion is formed directly and simultaneously as information is received.

Characteristically the crowd always functions at the perception stage of awareness-development,[76] while the behavior of the public which is expressed in public opinion, results from discussion among individuals who assume opposing positions. This discussion is based upon the presentation of facts.[77]

Fact is a new concept. Although the logical meaning of this word is not discussed here, its social-psychological meaning must be clarified. The process of reciprocal communication among the social animals has already been investigated. The unconscious reaction of one animal to an object it sees serves as signal and suggestion for the reactions of the other animals. This assumes that the object has the same meaning for all members of the group; otherwise it would be impossible to explain how communication would occur.

Where groups such as a public exist, and where objects have different meanings for different individuals, a new method of communication is necessary. This consists of resolving the object, the event, or whatever it might be, into its elements. These elements, in turn, can be objects, events, or elements of perception, but they

76 Sidis, *Psychology of Suggestion*, p. 296.

77 Precisely as reflection in individuals "assumes the existence of unconscious thinking," it must also be so assumed that when a social group passes to consultation and discussion, certain commonly known facts are present to which the discussion can be related.

Compare Windelband, *Präludien*, "Denken und Nachdenken."

must have the same meaning for all members of the group. These elements which have the same meaning for all members of the group can then be regarded as facts.

When this method of communication is used, it is possible to define and describe objects and events which have different values and meanings for various individuals and to make them accessible to all.[78] In a store that sells cigars, it can be established as a fact that the cigars offered are light colored, smell pleasant, and cost twenty-five cents. So far, these cigars are the same for both buyer and seller. However, they have two completely different meanings since the seller wants to dispose of them, and the buyer wants to smoke them. The real cigar now has different meanings for different individuals, while the cigar which has the same meaning for everyone must be viewed as an ideal construction.[79]

The public functions in such a world of objects having an ideal construction. It is characteristic of the nature of the public that a separation exists between the subjective and objective standpoints from which objects in the world can be viewed. Although these objects are definable and intelligible in the same way for all members of the public, they have different values for different individuals. Through the process which takes place within the public, the various attitudes of the different individuals conflict with and clarify each other. This results in a position which is suitable to the group as a whole. Only when the group itself is viewed as a subject, as one which takes positions and acts as an entity, can it become the object of a social-psychological explanation.[80]

78 Münsterberg, *Grundzüge*, pp. 298ff.

79 Stout, *A Manual of Psychology*, p. 313. "The external world as an ideal construction is a social product. It must therefore be independent of the individual subject in the same manner and in the same degree as social organization in general is independent of its individual members. There is thus introduced a new factor in the constitution of external reality—the social factor."

Compare Royce, *Studies of Good and Evil*, "Selfconsciousness, Social Consciousness and Nature," pp. 198ff.

80 Münsterberg, *Grundzüge*, pp. 99f. "Also the human group as such can appear as the carrier of psychic experience. The recognition and the will of national, economic, religious or kinship groups are no less real

It is a mistake to view public opinion as one which is acceptable to each individual member of the public to the same degree. It is much more an opinion or an attitude which is external to every individual and which is viewed as something objective. Precisely because public opinion is seen as the product of individual critical attitudes, it expresses itself variously in different individuals.

There is more. Other products of this critical behavior have been encountered, for example, prestige and the price of goods. What further characterizes the public is that the different viewpoints of different individuals are seen as subjective. The recognition of subjective viewpoints was first encountered historically in the Greek Enlightenment, and it is precisely this which characterizes the public and differentiates it from certain other kinds of groups, such as the crowd and the sect.[81] Along with the Greeks'

---

than the mental functions of the single fellow man. . . . When in historical reality a dependence is felt on social feeling and judgments, and when account is taken of the attitude of the national character, then the reality of an opposing social subject is not at all perceived as a complex of individuals, just as in everyday life fellow man is not perceived as a complex of cells. If the motives for recognizing the social subject are transferred to the language of psychology, then it is necessary to begin by perceiving many single individuals; each description derives from these cells of the social body; but for real dependence and in actual practice, the whole is valid only as a whole. The real individual subject is thus not contained as a part of the real social subject, but both interpenetrate each other as different realities; and only when they are thought of as existing objects does the one become an element of the other."

81 Windelband, *Präludien*, "Ueber Sokrates," 1st ed., p. 61. "For the first time in history a people appears whose total conditions of life are influenced by intellectual education, a people who place the direction of their public affairs in the hands of superior intellects, a people, in one word, who raised education to an essential element of its national existence. . . . At the same time that this education filtered through the Athenian population, the roots with which the individual had grown up in the soil of general consciousness were loosened, and he learned to follow his own judgment. This is the people who might be said to have discovered freedom, the freedom of the individual who wants to look and think for himself, who rejects authority, who dissolves his heaven into atoms, who declares himself to be the measure of all things, and projects himself as a self-defining atom of the world."

recognition of the value and significance of these subjective standpoints, there arose a desire to interpret and explain individual experience from a supra-individual, that is, a normative, perspective.[82]

It has been seen that this supra-individual perspective, along with the emergence of the public, is accepted as long as discussion, the only way of developing public opinion, is based on facts. Facts are elements of concrete reality having the same validity for all people, or at least for all members of the group. If these facts take the place of concrete reality, an ideally constructed object results which is equally acceptable for all members of the group. At the same time, the concrete reality to which the object is related has a different meaning for every member of the group.

It is seen that objects and events of the outer world always have different meanings for people as soon as they become aware of themselves; for "self-conscious" in the sense used here means differentiating oneself as a feeling and willing individual from other feeling and willing individuals.[83] At the very point, however, where individual interests and viewpoints diverge, practical life demands a definition and interpretation of objects and events in the outer world that is acceptable to all. Thus the need for a purely theoretical interpretation of things arises, one that is free from individual values.

Within the public, the practical and the theoretical behavior

82 Windelband, *Geschichte der Philosophie*, p. 54. "The question of whether there is something universally valid is the problem of the anthropological period of Greek philosophy or of the Greek enlightenment."

83 Royce, *Studies of Good and Evil*, "Consciousness and Nature," p. 215. "*My* opinion means, in general my opinion as contrasted with opinions which I attribute to other men. My private experience means, primarily, whatever nobody else but myself has experienced, and is therefore defined by contrast with the conception of what everybody else has experienced. . . . Take all this other experience out of my conception, and forthwith I lose all means of becoming conscious of my experience as mine, or of knowing what I mean either by my whole individuality or by my present Ego."

Compare Fichte, *Grundlage des Naturrechts*, *Sämtliche Werke*, pt. 2, vol. 1, p. 8.

of the group separate. It is not as if the "practical impulse" were completely missing in the theoretical attitude. For just as ethical-political impulses were the source of the first attempts to establish a knowledge which laid claim to a general validity among the variety of opinions,[84] so the practical impulse exerts its influence in the sciences. This occurs because the answers that sciences supply to their problems are predetermined not only by the given material but also by the way questions are posed.[85]

The public's attitudes are characteristically two-sided. The "being" of things, their meaning which is accepted as identical for all members of the group, and the "value" of things, which is different for all members, diverge as soon as a public comes into existence, while in the crowd "being" and "value" coincide. In attempting to base its practical behavior upon abstract views, and to formulate its will by counsel and discussion, the public again subjects itself to abstract norms. They are the necessary preconditions for the public's existence, because "the purely abstract man can exist beyond good and evil, but never beyond the true and the false."[86] Once accepted, the abstract norms function as a new force in collective life, and it is precisely this new force which is active in the public but not in the crowd.[87]

The public attempts to judge and determine individual evaluations from a supra-individual viewpoint. Characteristically, however, the public never reaches this viewpoint. What is lacking is

84 Windelband, *Geschichte der Philosophie*, p. 74.

85 Compare Rickert, *Der Gegenstand der Erkenntnis*; Windelband, *Präludien*, p. 29.

86 Rickert, *Der Gegenstand der Erkenntnis*, p. 90.

87 Windelband, *Präludien*, "Normen und Naturgesetze," p. 271. "If the consciousness of the norms—without increasing the empirical vitality and power of self-preservation in its carrier—is not only maintained in the history of man, but is intensified, deepened, and refined in various ways, then this must be caused by a direct and independent force which is not influenced by any secondary effect. This force is inherent in the consciousness of the norms as such; once it becomes dominant, it raises the conscience to a psychological power which appears as a new factor in psychic life. Only then has man understood the true essence and psychological meaning of norms."

the recognition of practical norms—the acceptance of law.[88] Public opinion is not accepted as a norm by members of the group. The individuals interacting within the public do not behave as beings who are independent and mutually invested with authority. The public is not a law-giving group. The opinion through which the public controls its individual members is a purely psychological product without any normative validity. Unlike public opinion, political laws cannot be viewed as psychological products, for they are also valid when they no longer function as natural powers in the collective consciousness.[89]

The development of these norms can perhaps be psychologically explained, but their validity is not accounted for in this way.[90] Public opinion presents only a part of the changing psychological conditions of the group. Laws are based on a solid tradition, on a mental perspective which can never be equated with the changing conditions of the group. This mental perspective of the group is called the general will.

88 Fichte, *Grundlage des Naturrechts*, *Sämtliche Werke*, pt. 2, vol. 1, p. 8. "Whatever the procedure might be in this formulation of the concept of law, I imagine it so. I assume myself to be rational, that is, free. The idea of freedom is present in this matter. I imagine other free beings in the same undifferentiated act. According to this, and using my imagination, I depict a sphere for the freedom in which several beings share. I do not grant myself all the freedom which I have set forth because I assume the presence of other free beings and must assign them a part of it. I limit myself in my possession of freedom through the fact that I also leave freedom for others. According to this, the concept of law is the concept of the necessary relationships of free beings together."

89 Hegel, *Philosophie des Rechts*, sec. 318. "Public opinion deserves to be equally despised and respected, despised for its concrete consciousness and expression, respected for its essential basis that is dimly apparent in that concrete presence."

90 Windelband, *Präludien*, "Normen und Naturgesetze," p. 214.

3

THE GENERAL WILL

I

THE CONCEPT of the general will enters modern philosophy for the first time in Rousseau's discussion about the "Volonté de tous."[1] It is true that Hobbes and Locke had already presented similar ideas. Hobbes, for example, argued that the state was a "real entity" and should be viewed as a person; but "real" in this sense can only mean that the state is the bearer of the unified power of those individuals united within it, for the state is based upon an agreement, it is an "artificial person."[2] "Person" should likewise be understood as a legal construct, the bearer of the rights given up by the individuals.[3] For Hobbes there is no "moral person" recognizing in its own consciousness the power of a higher law; the general will is so unlike the "real" will of individuals, that the state comes into existence only after individual wills subordinate themselves to the will of the ruler and accept his commands unconditionally.[4]

For man, the state of nature is a condition of mutual hostility, a *bellum omnium contra omnes*. Only when this natural state is abolished does the State come into being. With the formation of the State, individual wills are surrendered to the will of the collectivity which is represented through the person and will of the ruler. This general will always exists as something external to the

1 Bosanquet, *The Philosophical Theory of the State*, p. 13.

2 Hobbes, *Leviathan*, pt. 2, chap. 17, and Foreword. Compare also Kistiakowski, *Gesellschaft und Einzelwesen*, p. 10.

3 Bosanquet, *Theory of the State*, p. 93.

4 Ibid., p. 104; Windelband, *Geschichte der neueren Philosophie*, 1:154.

individuals. According to Hobbes there is no self-government, since rule is always and necessarily coercive.[5]

This doctrine of the State's permanent opposition to individuals, of the State as an external power limiting individual freedom, appears elsewhere, even in the writings of those men who in other points do not agree with Hobbes, such as Goodwin, John Stuart Mill, and Spencer.[6] The doctrine received its classic expression in Bentham's statement: "Government is a necessary evil."[7] Common to all these writers is the assumption that there is a complete separation existing between the individual and the State. However, this is not to be understood as in Hegel's theory where the individual finds his true self and his freedom only in the State. It means instead that the individual must always renounce a part of his freedom to the State, as much as is necessary for securing the same freedom for all other individuals.[8]

Rousseau's writings represent the historical transition from the doctrine of Hobbes and Locke to that of the general will as it appears in the political philosophy of Hegel.[9] Locke wrote his "Essay on Civil Government" primarily to justify the English Revolution.[10] He diverged from Hobbes's doctrine insofar as he believed that the general will was ultimately based in the community and was only taken over temporarily by ruler and government for the representative exercise of power.[11] The will which actually exerts its influence in the community is thus not the will of the col-

5 Janet, *Histoire de la science politique*, 2:182.

6 Bonar, *Philosophy and Political Economy*, pp. 199ff; Bosanquet, *Theory of the State*, pp. 60ff., 69ff.

7 Bentham, *Principles of Legislation*, p. 48.

8 Mill, *On Liberty*, chap. 4.

9 Bosanquet, *Theory of the State*, p. 13. "For it is Rousseau who stands midway between Hobbes and Locke on the one hand and Kánt and Hegel on the other. . . . and he bequeathed to his successors the task of substituting for mere words and fictions of contract, nature, and original freedom, the idea of the common life of an essentially social being, expressing and sustaining the human will at its best."

10 Janet, *Histoire de la science politique*, 2:199.

11 Locke, *Essay on Civil Government*, chap. 7.

lectivity, but that of the sovereign who exercises his own will under the conditions of the constitution. This transfer of sovereignty to the king and parliament is always conditional and can be recalled as soon as the conditions are not fulfilled.[12] For Locke the general will was not an "actual" will, but only the position of individuals who agreed with or rejected the actions of the government; he viewed these individuals not as an entity but as separate persons. "Thus for Hobbes," Bosanquet states, "it can be said that the political unity lies in a will which is real but not common (not a general will); it is namely the will of the sovereign. For Locke, on the other hand, this unity lies in a will which although general, is not real."[13]

Rousseau often used the language of Locke and Hobbes; in general his writings appear to vacillate between the earlier concept of social unity which places unity above and outside the circle of individual volitions, and the later concept which locates this unity in a general will existing in real and substantial opinions instead of in a common agreement.[14] The relapse into earlier doctrines is clearest where Rousseau attempted to formulate the social mechanism through which the state was to form this general will. For this, he prescribed a relentless regime of public meetings which were to embody the sovereignty of the state.[15]

In presenting his doctrine, Rousseau also used the historical fiction of the social contract. He treats this "contract" as a universal and constitutive relationship; only when it is accepted is the State

12 Ibid., chaps. 13 and 18.

13 Bosanquet, *Theory of the State*, p. 104.

14 Ritchie, *Natural Rights*, p. 49.

15 Rousseau, *Du Contrat social*, bk. 3, chap. 15. "Sovereignty cannot be represented for the same reason that it can not be alienated; its essence lies in the general will, and will cannot be represented. . . . Any law not ratified by the people themselves is not a law. English people consider themselves free; they are strongly mistaken. It is only so during the election of members of parliament. As soon as they are elected, the English are slaves, that is, nothing."

Compare Ritchie, *Natural Rights*, p. 50; Windelband, *Geschichte der neueren Philosophie*, p. 436.

called into being.[16] Where this concept of the social contract is most generally formulated, it means nothing more than the mutual recognition of individuals as persons who possess rights and duties. Here the social contract is the formal expression of the normative consciousness which constitutes the prerequisite for concrete relationships between individuals within the political body.[17]

On the other hand, Rousseau views man's original existence prior to his entering into social bonds with others as a condition of natural freedom. In earlier writings he speaks of society as if its formation meant the annulment of individual freedom.[18] But in *The Social Contract* he contrasts the natural freedom of the individual, innocent of social bonds, with the new freedom that man first gains within the State.[19] Here Rousseau's teachings oppose

16 Rousseau, *Du Contrat social*, bk. 1, chap. 8. "This transition from the state of nature to the civil state produces a very remarkable transformation in man. Justice is substituted for instinct in his conduct, and his actions take on morality, which was lacking before then. It is only when the voice of duty replaces physical impulse, and law replaces appetite, that man, who up to then only looked after himself, finds himself forced to act upon other principles and to consult his reason before listening to his desires."

17 Windelband, *Präludien*, "Was ist Philosophie?" p. 49. "The validity of the normative consciousness as the absolute measure for logical, ethical, and esthetic judgments, lies as an inevitable assumption at the basis of all man's higher functions, and especially at the basis of those functions which are the product of social culture and have as their content the production and preservation of that which stands above the desires of the individual."

18 Rousseau, *Discours sur l'origine de l'inégalité parmi les hommes*, pt. 1. "It is thus the same with man; while becoming socialized and enslaved, he becomes weak, fearful, and cringing."

19 Rousseau, *Du Contrat social*, bk. 1, chap. 8. "What man loses in the social contract is his natural liberty and an unlimited right to everything that tempts him and that he can obtain; what he gains is civil liberty along with ownership of all that he possesses. . . . moral liberty can be added accordingly to his gains within the civil state; only this can make man truly master of himself, for domination by the appetites alone is slavery; and obedience to the law that one has prescribed for himself is freedom."

Compare Hegel, *Philosophie des Rechts*, sec. 258.

Hegel's, since Hegel considered the so-called natural freedom existing before the creation of the moral individual to be exactly the opposite of freedom.[20] Freedom in Hegel's sense is only attained by the moral individual who aspires to a rational ideal; freedom can therefore only be realized within the State.[21]

The essential element in Rousseau's teaching is his separation of "general will" (*volonté général*) and the "will of everyone" (*volonté de tous*), which indicates his progress beyond Locke. The will of everyone must not be interpreted as an expression of the general will.[22] Coincidental agreement among the empirical wills of individuals does not constitute the essence of the general will. Instead, it can be said to exist only when a universal goal is desired and when this desire takes the form of a law which is equally valid for everyone at all times. Only when the individual subjects himself to a general law and refrains from obeying momentary drives, is the decision resulting from a popular vote identical with the general will.[23]

It would be easy to conclude that the individual will is the same as the general will, or at least could be seen as its subjective expression. Hegel's development of this thought will be discussed below. But for Rousseau, this interpretation was impossible, since

20 Hegel, *Philosophie des Rechts*, sec. 194.

21 W. Wallace, *Lectures and Essays*, "Person and Personality," p. 266. "Personality, in short, is a quality of the human being that expresses his moral nature. And the moral nature of man lies in his being subordinate to a general law, or being a member of a community, in which he forms an integral part and performs a function. Or, personality, like morality, only belongs to man in so far as, though a physical individual, he is implicitly universal."

22 Rousseau, *Du Contrat social*, bk. 2, chap. 3. "It follows from the above that the general will is always right, and that it always tends toward the public good. But it does not follow that the deliberations of the people always result in good; this is not always understood. The people can never be corrupted, but they can often be deceived and thus they only appear to desire what is evil. There is often a great difference between the 'will of everyone' and the 'general will.' The latter only concerns what is of common interest. The former expresses private interests; it is only the sum of individual desires."

23 Ibid., bk. 2, chap. 6.

he retained the old separation of nation (the people) and the government. As a result, his doctrine (as well as Locke's) does not mention a specific organ for forming the general will. The government is not this organ; according to Locke it retains sovereignty only temporarily, while Rousseau considered it to be simply an administrative committee.[24] In order to define the general will, it is necessary to resort to the general consensus of citizens.[25]

The concept of the general will, which is only briefly sketched out in Rousseau's doctrine, was then taken up and further developed in classic German philosophy. Its most complete expression occurs in Hegel's teaching of the objective spirit.[26] Under this term, Hegel reunited the two aspects of the general will, one moral, the other legal, which Kant's somewhat one-sided insistence upon

24 Locke, *Civil Government*, chap. 2, sec. 22; Bosanquet, *Theory of the State*, p. 105. "Locke feels that actual government is a trust and that the ultimate supreme power remains in the community as a whole. . . . But the trust is conditional and theoretically revocable; the ultimate supreme power is in the community at large, which may withdraw the trust if its conditions are violated. Of course, no determinate means of doing this in a lawful manner is or can be suggested and therefore the will of the people is not expressed by Locke as a real or actual will."

Rousseau, *Du Contrat social*, bk. 3, chap. 1.

25 Bosanquet, *Theory of the State*, p. 116. "Now all this makes it clear that in endeavouring to point out the sign of the general will, Rousseau is really enthroning the will of all. . . . By reducing the machinery for the expression of the common good to the isolated and unassisted judgment of the members of the whole body of citizens, Rousseau is ensuring the exact reverse of what he professes to aim at. He is appealing from the organized life, institutions and selected capacity of a nation to that nation regarded as an aggregate of isolated individuals. And, therefore, he is enthroning as sovereign, not the national mind, but that aggregate of private interests and ideas, which he has himself described as the will of all."

26 Windelband, *Geschichte der neueren Philosophie*, 2:326ff. "Hegel's doctrine of the objective spirit includes in the widest sense the entire area to which the tasteless name of sociology is applied today. . . . The essence of the objective spirit is completed only when its outer and inner forms coincide. This synthesis of legality and morality was called public morality [*Sittlichkeit*] by Hegel; it is expressly differentiated from morality [*Moralität*]."

the autonomy of the individual had set into opposition. The autonomous will is the one that rises above the system of empirical drives and shapes itself solely by the law of reason. The highest moral law is: the individual should behave as if he wished that the maxims of his behavior would become general laws of nature.[27] But although this law is generally necessary and valid for all men, it is purely formal; for as Hegel emphasized, it demands nothing more than the formal accord of the individual with himself.[28] The individual yields to the law he must follow. The subjectivism of this concept is revealed in the doctrine that only the good will is good.[29] Kant's philosophy of law ascribed no inherent moral value to public institutions; this is the greatest difference between his philosophy of law and that of Hegel.

It is necessary to mention the special importance of Fichte's

27 Ibid., 2:116.

28 Hegel, *Philosophie des Rechts*, sec. 135. "As important as it is to emphasize the pure unconditional self-determination as the root of duty—through Kant's philosophy, knowledge of the will gained its secure basis and point of departure by reflection upon the infinite autonomy of the will—adherence to a purely moral standpoint which is not transformed into a conception of ethics reduces this gain to an empty formalism; it reduces the science of morals to mere talk of duty for its own sake. And from this last standpoint, no immanent doctrine of duty is possible. (Of course, something can be brought in from outside, and specific duties can be derived from this.) But from that definition of duty seen as the lack of contradiction, as the formal agreement with itself—this is nothing but confirmation of an abstract indefiniteness—specific duties cannot proceed. When a specific content for behavior is examined, the foregoing principle does not provide a criterion of whether it is or is not a duty. On the contrary, all wrong and immoral behavior can be justified in this manner."

29 Windelband, *Geschichte der neueren Philosophie*, 2:326. "It is a credit to Hegel's wisdom, that he treated ethics from an objective rather than a subjective standpoint. Precisely the subjectivism of Kant's and Fichte's moral philosophy has shown that the principle of ethics must be sought for at a level above the individual. Moral consciousness and moral legislation can never be derived from the individual 'I.' It is rooted instead in the relationship wherein the individual realizes he is subordinate to a general reason."

doctrine of State and law, for it provides the transition from the eighteenth-century to the nineteenth-century theory of the State; in other words, from the subjective concept of Kant's ethical norm to Hegel's objective interpretation.[30] For Fichte, it is the individual's duty to enact in particular the supra-individual will. "The voice of conscience, which shows everyone his particular duty, is the beam on which we emerge from the infinite and are established as individual and particular beings; this voice sets the limits of our personality; it is also our true primitive element, the basis and the ingredient of all our existences."[31]

The idea of the supra-individual life first appeared in the Kantian notion of "consciousness in general."[32] Although the concept revealed a complete break with Enlightenment philosophy, Fichte remained on the same ground as Hobbes insofar as his closed economic state presented the State simply as the sum of external conditions under which the individual could fulfill his destiny.[33] However, his concept of the State developed continually in the various forms of his teachings. Before publication of his essay on the "closed economic state," Fichte had already prided himself in being the first to conceive of the State as an organism.[34] Although the idea was already contained in his theory of morals, it was first clearly expressed in the *Talks to the German People:* the State

30 Windelband, *Fichtes Idee des deutschen Staates*, p. 9. "Where the previous century rationalized, this one wants to nationalize. Between these two stands Fichte—Janus-faced, he sounds the rousing cry to the future but still is filled with thoughts of the past."

31 Fichte, *Die Bestimmung des Menschen*, p. 299.

32 Windelband, *Geschichte der Philosophie*, pp. 445, 448.

33 Windelband, *Geschichte der neueren Philosophie*, 2:222. "As he [Fichte] published his *Grundlage des Naturrechts* in 1796, he still was formally under the influence of the 18th century. Out of the principle of the theory of science, he deduced the plurality of physically organized personalities, and he discovered that in outward community life, the freedom of every individual must be limited by that of all others. But when he viewed the State as the means for obtaining this, he applied its functions only to outer relationships and not to moral ends."

34 Fichte, *Grundlage des Naturrechts*, p. 209. Compare Wallace, *Lectures and Essays*, "The Relations of Fichte and Hegel to Socialism," p. 427.

is also an individual, it has a destiny which its actual existence serves to realize.[35]

It has already been noted that Hegel's doctrine of the objective spirit is the fullest development of Rousseau's original concept of the general will. In his *Philosophy of Law*, Hegel defined the State in the same sense as Fichte did in *Talks to the German People*—a sentient individual whose essence is a particular application of the general spirit; this spirit finds its actualization in world history.[36] Thus the State is not a work of art nor a simple ideal floating before the individuals in the society; instead it is something real, a sentient substance which has actualized itself in governmental institutions.[37]

Exactly as with the individual's real will, which is his essence, so also the State's real will is never identical with the empirical will but is only partially expressed in it. Therefore "the spirit of the nation does not speak out in the exchange of momentary opinions, nor in the arbitrariness of parliamentary leaders, but expresses itself instead in the stable structure which the State achieves through its continual development."[38]

Hegel believed that the ethical substance, which he called

35 Fichte, *Reden an die deutsche Nation*, p. 381. "In the higher meaning of the word, taken from the standpoint of a general spiritual world, this is a nation: the totality of people surviving with each other in society and perpetuating themselves continually, both physically and spiritually; it stands as a whole under a certain special divine law of development. It is the common quality of this special law which both in the eternal world, and thus also in the temporal one, binds this group of people into a totality that is natural and homogeneous."

Compare Windelband, *Geschichte der neueren Philosophie*, 2:224; Bosanquet, *Theory of the State*, p. 244.

36 Hegel, *Philosophie des Rechts*, sec. 258, Supplement. "Whether man knows it or not, this being (the State) actualizes itself as an independent power in which single individuals are only moments; the existence of the State is the march of God; its basis is the power of the intelligence actualizing itself as will."

Compare ibid., pt. 3, div. 3, p. 423.

37 Ibid., sec. 258. "The State is as the reality of the substantial will which is contained in the special self-consciousness raised to its universality; it is intelligence in and for itself."

38 Windelband, *Geschichte der neueren Philosophie*, 2:329.

morality and which is here identified with Rousseau's general will (*volonté général*), assumed three different forms. In the family, the general will assumes its immediate form, that of feeling and natural drive.[39] As long as the family is part of the State, the family is the natural form of society.[40] The unity seen here is direct; individual elements possess no independence in the face of the whole. "The right which the individual possesses on the basis of family unity, and which constitutes his life itself within this unity, emerges in the form of a right (only insofar as it is the abstract moment of the specific individuality) when the family is in the process of dissolving, and those who were members become independent people, both in their self-conception and in reality. In their separation, only the outer aspects of that which made them definite forces within the family is now preserved: possessions, nourishment, cost of education, etc."[41]

If the family is dissolved into its individual elements, so that in their separation members interact only in terms of external bonds, there results the form of society which Hegel called civil society.[42] In civil society individuals are conscious of their private interests wherever these are in conflict with the interests of other individuals.[43] Individuals thus become self-conscious; as their private interests press to the forefront and become the determining force of consciousness, a split develops between the individual and the totality, and the totality appears as something external and foreign to the individual. If a general consensus does exist among the members of civil society, it assures the form of the "will of everyone," for "in civil society everyone is his own end, everything else is nothing to him."[44]

It is characteristic of Hegel that he valued these forms of society in which individual differences appear, and that he saw

39 Hegel, *Philosophie des Rechts*, sec. 158.
40 Ibid., sec. 151.
41 Ibid., sec. 159.
42 Ibid., secs. 157, 184 and 238.
43 Ibid., sec. 184, Supplement.
44 Ibid., sec. 182.

them as an essential force in the development of the general will as it appears in the State.[45] The general will assumes the self-conscious form of reason only within the State.[46] It is precisely in the State that the general will consolidates the differences between individual elements that first appear in civil society. Because this occurs in the State, this form consists of the unity of differences.[47] It is not "the interests of individuals per se which stand as the final end of their unification," as is the case in civil society; instead, "unification itself is the true content and goal, and the destiny of the individuals is to lead a common existence. This substantive and universal life is the beginning and end of their further particular satisfaction, activity, and behavior."[48]

The concept of general will, as it appears perfected in Hegel's philosophy of the State, must be understood as a sentient substance; it appears subjectively within the individual consciousness in the form of conscience, and objectively in the form of mores.[49] The foundations of morality as well as the laws which the political community applies to itself are based upon this spiritual substance.

The general will is finally to be understood as the essence of all that which is valid for the social group, whether it is the family or the State, in contrast to that which operates continually in the collectivity as drives.[50] The concept of the general will in the

45 Ibid., sec. 187.

46 Ibid., sec. 258.

47 Ibid.

48 Ibid.

49 Bosanquet, *Theory of the State*, p. 93. "We find that the essence of human society consists in a common self, a life and a will, which belong to and are exercised by the society as such, or by the individuals in society as such; it makes no difference which expression we choose. This reality of this common self, in the action of the political whole, receives the name of the 'general will.' "

Ibid., p. 298. "In institutions, then, we have that meeting point of the individual minds which is the social mind. Rather let us say we have the ideal substance, which, as a universal structure, is the social, but in its differentiated cases is the individual mind."

Compare Windelband, *Präludien*, "Vom Prinzip der Moral," p. 308.

50 Bosanquet, *Theory of the State*, p. 39. "A strong sentiment, as

writings of Hegel and others before and after him is not basically sociological, but ethical-legal.[51] An attempt to transfer this notion of the general will into social psychology resulted in one of the many controversial problems of the last century, for the question of the general will and its relationship to individuals in the group ran parallel to the problem of the relationship of the soul to the body.[52]

From the viewpoint of this study, the problem is purely epistemological; it concerns the question of whether psychology is to be viewed as a purely natural and phenomenological science, or not. Basically, the general will would not be considered an object of social psychology, because it could never be equated with any of its manifestations. On the other hand, since the general will exists as a historic structure in society, it would have to be viewed as a product and formative element in the empirical process of society.[53] This question does not need to be answered here, for in any case the reality of the general will remains unquestioned, and that is sufficient for the present aim, the definition of the concepts "crowd" and "public."

---

such, is a mere fact, a mere force; and as such the sociologist regards it; a law involves the pretention to will what is just, and is therefore a sentiment and something more, vis., the point of view of social good." Kistiakowski, *Gesellschaft und Einzelwesen*, p. 154. "In all research into social processes, it is very important to differentiate between the general spirit which forms a totality or a collectivity to which the individual spirits are related as parts, and the general spirit which, as norm or laws, controls all individual spirits, and represents, in a special sense, a generic term for all its effects on individual consciousnesses. The difference is already clear from the fact that moral-legal order or norms always remain the same for all individuals who originate in the same society, regardless of their number; on the other hand, patriotic or other social feelings or desires are highly dependent in their social meaning and effect upon the number of individuals."

51 Windelband, *Präludien*, 1st ed., "Normen und Naturgesetze," p. 176.

52 Windelband, *Geschichte der Philosophie*, pp. 516ff., 529.

53 Münsterberg, *Grundzüge*, pp. 93 and 203. Windelband, *Präludien*, 1st ed., "Normen und Naturgesetze," p. 246.

II

The end of this work has been reached, and it is necessary to summarize what is most relevant for the concepts of crowd and public. It has been seen that the concept of reciprocity (sympathy or imitation) does not suffice for a definition of society, since reciprocity also occurs in "the war of all against all" (panic). The notion of society implies that the people it includes form a more or less permanent unity and are capable of acting as such. When society is viewed as such an entity, it assumes the category of a reality. The question is: of what does social reality consist?

The reality of society cannot be found in its external appearances because the perception of society is not limited to its external phenomena, and in addition, society does not present a homogeneous whole. The so-called organic theory was an attempt to understand society as a perceivable entity, but this idea was never seriously developed and always led to confusion. However, this should not discourage anyone from conceiving of society as a reality.

An individual's own personality consists of just such a stable combination of qualities, and this combination assumes a reality even though it is never visually perceived. What is called the personality is perceived outwardly in actions, inwardly as impulses and drives. Viewed as a cohesive whole, these impulses and drives can be called the will. The will is never identical with individual impulses and drives as they emerge in the consciousness; instead, these impulses and drives are the manifestation of the will.

It is possible to speak of a general will in the same way. General will does not merely refer to the interaction and reciprocal formation of individual wills, but more to the existence of a permanent relationship between them. Because of this relationship, people who join together at different times can be regarded not only as the same people, but also as the same society.

The general will, which is first formulated in the mores, must not be considered a third element, something apart from the individual wills, but as what is essential in them. The general will is distinguished from the drives and instincts of single individuals only when it is violated, that is, when the individual's drives or actions take a course opposed to it. In this way the moral element, which was previously expressed only as a drive, emerges as a norm in the collective consciousness.

The feelings and behavior which are awakened within the collectivity by the immoral action of one individual must be viewed as the expression of the general will—a kind of evaluation of the offensive action. A similar evaluation of immoral behavior will occur in the consciousness of the offender himself. Such an evaluation of personal behavior is expressed in feelings of embarrassment, shame, regret, etc.—or in a self-judgment. In its clearest form, this process of self-judgment is called conscience.

A double misunderstanding must be avoided here: In the first place, the general will must not be equated with the feeling and ideas actually controlling the collectivity at every moment. Nor is it simply what is active in the collective consciousness as drive and natural force. Instead, the general will is *what is morally valid for the collectivity.* Thus the differentiation between the "will of everyone" and the "general will," between empirical and normative collective will.

Secondly, it is incorrect to think that the collective consciousness which judges immoral action is determined only by personal and individual interests. If this were so, the judgment of the collectivity would have to be expressed so: "This action is opposed to our interests, therefore it is wrong." In contrast, each naive judgment of an action—if ever expressed—states: "This action does not agree with the mores, therefore it is bad." It is only when an attempt is made to justify this judgment from a philosophical outlook based on individual sense perceptions, that it is necessary to understand individually these actions of the collectivity.

In order to avoid the difficulties of explaining moral judgments on an individualist-sensualist basis, the concept of sympathy has been adopted. It has been seen that sympathetic imitation in itself is a purely formal process, the means through which men are able to experience the feelings of other people. Only in this way does the inner life of others become a motive for personal behavior.

However, the images in the consciousness of the individuals involved are only partially determined by the process of reciprocity and are not always well intended. Pleasure in another person's misfortunes [*Schadenfreude*] is as much a product of the process of sympathetic imitation as is pity. The fact that the sense of norms is not determined by sympathetic feelings is shown by the acts of pity which are frequently committed with the knowledge that it is wrong to do so. The ability to empathize at all with others assumes that something in common exists. Thus in spite of empathy, people know what right actions are. This shows that there is an element in human consciousness which is determined neither by individual sense perceptions nor through the reflected sense perceptions of other people.

Equally without basis is the claim that even if the general will cannot be equated with the sympathetic interaction of individual feelings, it must nevertheless be viewed genetically as the product of such interaction. This again is true only insofar as the sympathetic interpenetration and reconciliation of individual feelings is the precondition of a collective action. For it is always the necessity of a common action to protect common possessions that has produced a collective spirit in men.

The necessity of collective action has had other effects. Whenever a division developed within the group, it has forced individuals to examine and evaluate their individual tendencies and interests with an eye to the aims of the collectivity. It is this collective purpose, again, which has become so established in the general will that it does not simply hover in front of people as an ideal, but acts as an ideal force to inspire and drive them on.

The general psychological characteristics of social groups are: (1) reciprocity, that is, the mutual affecting and reconciling of human drives, and (2) a general will which is first expressed as a collective force overpowering and assimilating all individual drives. Existing at times as a norm, it opposes the transient individual feelings and drives of the collectivity.

The next question is: How are the many kinds of groups to be differentiated which appear and dissolve in endless variety against the background of human existence?

In spite of their great variety, this study separates groups into two classes. First, there is the category of sects, castes, classes, and groups which serve any special purpose whatsoever. These are all highly varied among themselves and must be further classified. The only characteristic they have in common is that they are not isolated, or in existence only for themselves. The existence of each group is based on that of other groups different from it. A political party, for example, assumes the existence of other political parties. Without the others, a single party would be inconceivable, and these parties are opposed in such a manner that no person can simultaneously be a member of two of them.

But the political parties, just like all other groups which have developed within society in order to serve some special interest or other, or to carry out a social function, presume the existence of a collectivity in which they are viewed as the parts. Their aims and the forces which influence them are only the particular manifestations of a general will which, for its part, attains fuller expression in the political organization of a State or in national cults.

Crowd and public are different from all of these. They represent the second type of association, which grows out of and beyond the others, and they serve to bring individuals out of old ties and into new ones. Compared with those social structures just discussed, crowd and public differ strikingly from them. The historical element which plays such an important role for the other groups is partially or completely absent for the crowd as well as the public. Instead, the crowd and the public reveal the processes through which new groups are formed, although they are not yet conscious of themselves as groups. The individuals in a crowd or a public lack a common tradition, so they have no basis for viewing themselves as a permanent collectivity. For example, people gather in a public square; they converse, exchange opinions, and then go their separate ways; the intimate sense of personal and spiritual contact and the awakened feelings and interests which united them for a short time now dissolve. This is the simplest form that a crowd or a public can take.

In contrast, there is the situation where a number of people gather frequently and regularly. Here the mood which was dominant at the first encounter is invoked again at the second, third, fourth, etc., union, and in this way customs and traditions are built. A group so formed finally becomes conscious of its temporal duration, and with this consciousness the group differentiates more or less between itself and other people. The tradition formed this way supplies the material for a norm which is to regulate the group. When the group finally differentiates itself from others in order to defend its tradition, the goal of the process is reached whose beginning was seen at work in crowd formation. The group is now changed; the collective consciousness assumes the normative form; in other words, the will of the group, which formerly operated as a collective force dominating the drives of individuals, develops into norm and regulation.

The relationship between crowd and public and the other social groups can now be seen. From a standpoint of form, or conceptually, crowd and public precede the other groups; actually, they occur later—they are frequently the forms that the other groups take to transform themselves into a new, undefined whole. In addition, they are the forms individuals belonging to different established groups use to make new groupings. Thus as crowd and public appear in modern life, they assume the prior existence of other groups which functionally express the varied, divided interests of men. Wherever a new interest asserts itself amid those already existing, a crowd or a public simultaneously develops; and through this union of groups, or certain individuals from among them, a new social form for the new interests is created. In Europe a public reaching beyond the boundaries of states and nationalities has formed; and the general statement can be made that a public always develops where the interests of people, whether political or economic, come into conflict and seek to reconcile themselves. Further, it is precisely this contact and reciprocal adjustment of opinion which has given rise to a tradition reaching beyond the boundaries of states and nationalities, a tradition containing the kernel of a norm and of legislation which is international.

It is not the content of the collective consciousness, but rather its form, that separates crowd and public from the other kinds of groups. Crowd and public are dominated by a collective force, but this kind of collective will has not yet assumed the form of a norm; therefore it cannot be viewed as general will in the historical sense of the word, but instead as an empirical preliminary stage to it. Neither the crowd nor the public recognizes itself as a whole, nor do they attempt to determine their own actions. No regulations, conscious control, or self-consciousness exists. Crowd and public are defined only by the conditions of reciprocal interaction, and therefore they cannot define themselves as do all other groups. For example, admission to a normal eating club is always bound up with certain formalities in which the new member virtually obligates himself to adapt to the mood of the group and respect the existing tradition.

In these respects crowd and public are alike; their difference is based on the conditions under which they develop. Entrance to the crowd depends on the simplest conditions imaginable, namely, possessing the ability to feel and empathize. Admittedly, choice and selection occur even under these conditions, but this is purely psychological, and the individual himself is unaware of it. There is also a control here, but it is purely psychological and not normative. The individual experiences the collective will as his own internal drive.

The conditions under which one enters the public are somewhat more exacting. Not only the ability to feel and empathize is required, but also the ability to think and reason with others. That does not mean that a person is forced to bow to some procedural regulation or other; only the norms of logic must be accepted unconditionally.

There is another difference between crowd and public: the public expresses criticism. Within the public, opinions are divided. When the public ceases to be critical, it dissolves or is transformed into a crowd. This provides the essential characteristic differentiating the crowd from the public: The crowd submits to the influence of a collective drive which it obeys without criticism. The public, in contrast—precisely because it is composed of individuals with different opinions—is guided by prudence and rational reflection. However, it cannot be ignored that like the crowd, the public is to some degree influenced by the collective drive. But within the public, this collective drive has found individual expression in the various parties or individuals. The insight gained through criticism and the resulting explanation of the drive controlling the public is called "public opinion."

If an attempt is made to define crowd and public according to the form in which control is exercised, it is clear that they are, properly speaking, the only forms of society which can be called individualistic. Again, a difference between crowd and public must be recognized. Only in the crowd does anarchy in its purest form exist. As members of a public, people are at least controlled by the norms of logic. The ultimate tyranny, as Max Stirner has already noted, is that of the concept.

While crowd and public are differentiated so that in the former the instincts dominate, and in the latter reason prevails (suggesting that the public is a higher form of society than the crowd), one point must not be overlooked: this differentiation refers only to the form of the collective consciousness, and not to its content. This distinction is purely logical and cannot be viewed as a value difference.

Finally, the decisive difference between crowd and public must be emphasized: in the crowd, both the theoretical and the practical norm are implicit in the collective impulse, while in the public—precisely because the individuals have different opinions—the two norms diverge. Here individuals are dominated by the theoretical norm even when the practical norm is held up before them as an ideal attainable only through action and discussion.

II. Other Essays

1

SOCIAL PLANNING AND HUMAN NATURE

I. *Human Nature*

GRAHAM WALLAS in his little treatise on *Human Nature and Politics* makes, by way of introduction, casual reference to a personal experience which suggests the nature of the problem with which his book and this paper are mainly concerned. He says: "In my last election I noticed that two of my canvassers, when talking over the day's work, used independently the phrase, 'It *is* a queer business.' "

On another occasion, he adds, he heard much the same words used by professional political agents "whose efficiency depends on their seeing electoral facts without illusion." Still later, in talking over his experience with members of the Paris Municipal Council, he "seemed to detect in some of them a good humored disillusionment with regard to the workings of a democratic electoral system."

The notion that the task, which a democratic scheme of government imposes, of winning every now and then an election, is a queer and baffling business, is one that is likely to follow a more intimate acquaintance with practical politics anywhere. It is based in part no doubt on a lack of understanding of the political process itself, but is due in part, also, to the natural optimism of mankind that leads one, in the ardor of promoting a political cause, to expect too much of human nature and sometimes leave it altogether out of the reckoning.

Reprinted with permission from *Publication of the American Sociological Society*, August 1935, pp. 19–28.

In order to get the attention of the voter it is necessary to capture his imagination. In order to make him move and march it is necessary to have music and banners, and an immense amount of (what is popularly described as) ballyhoo.

It is probable, also, that the notion that electioneering is a queer business merely reflects a kind of general disenchantment that eventually overtakes the man who starts out to inspire and lead the masses, and discovers that his real task is to follow and try to manage them.

Practical politicians do not often discuss in public the mysteries of their profession. When they do there is often a note of cynicism in what they say, suggesting that their present realism had not been achieved without the loss of certain illusions.

Candid accounts of what actually happens behind the scenes in the conduct of political parties and in the management of labor organizations are likely to be disconcerting and disillusioning to the innocent bystander.

It is notorious that lawyers have a poor opinion of juries and they are likely in private conversation to be most enlivening when they are describing the personal eccentricities of judges on the bench. These anecdotes certainly throw an interesting light upon judicial procedure but one can detect in them that same good humored, not to say irreverent, disillusionment to which Graham Wallas refers.

Other professions, which have to deal with the public as individuals, that is, in succession, or in the mass, are not exempt. Physicians know that, in actual practice, success depends not merely on professional skill but upon a certain amount of tact in dealing with the frailties of human nature.

Doctors have to tolerate a good deal of medical superstition in their patients. They have discovered that black pills are best for white folk and white pills for black; that in provincial communities it is still advisable to wear whiskers; and that in general it is important to take human nature into the reckoning.

In the newspaper profession one has to distinguish between the editorial writer and the reporter. The former, when he takes himself seriously, as he sometimes does, is likely to conceive of himself as a minor prophet, or at any rate as a leader and inspirer of public opinion. The news editor and reporter, on the other hand, think more realistically about the public and the profession. It is their business to get and print the news, and make the public read it. Most newspaper men have a poor opinion of the public.

Arthur Brisbane, one of the most distinguished members of the profession, is reported to have said, in explaining the policy of the Hearst papers, that the public is like a baby in the bath. You have to drum on the bathtub to keep it amused while you labor to improve its condition.

The principle upon which the newspaper actually operates is one that was casually enunciated by my friend Alexander Johnson. Someone asked him how it was he was able to speak to, and interest, all sorts and conditions of people. He said: "Well, the fact is, I was once head of an institution for the feebleminded. I had to speak every Sunday morning. I found that if you can speak to the feebleminded you can speak to anyone."

I am recording these somewhat disquieting observations upon the actual workings of our social institutions, not because they suggest that reform is urgent and necessary—as no doubt it is—but rather because they indicate the kind of problem that arises at the end of the political process rather than at the beginning, the problem, namely—human nature being what it is—of making any social program, no matter how well planned, work.

The thing that makes business, politics, and human intercourse generally, exciting and chancy, is the presence of this more or less incalculable human factor.

The man who makes a discovery; invents some new gadget—anything, idea or artifact—designed to add something to the sum total of existing cultural values discovers that it is not enough to produce something of value. He has to sell it.

One reason that electioneering seems a queer business is probably due to the fact that the candidate attempts to deal with the electorate in accordance with the democratic assumption that every voter is a rational human being, quite capable of acting wisely, independently, and in the public interest, if only he is afforded the temporary protection and seclusion of a voting booth.

He discovers, however, that most men are timid, irrational, and sentimental creatures, controlled by all sorts of personal interests and irrational affections and antipathies.

Graham Wallas's statement of the matter is that political thinking in the past has assumed a degree of intellectuality in mankind that mankind never really possessed. The human nature with which he is concerned in the volume to which I have referred is that pre-rational and nonrational behavior which complicates the political processes everywhere, and on which the tactics of practical politicians are based.

Other writers, many, perhaps, even in recent times, James Bryce among them, have recognized that political science is based finally on a knowledge of human nature. In his *Modern Democracies* he remarks that in human societies there is one "constant," one element or factor which is practically always the same and the basis of all the so-called societies. This is human nature itself.

This is, as George Catlin who quotes it remarks, a highly ambiguous statement, but it does recognize the fact that has been recently recognized elsewhere that the social sciences, including economics and politics, are fundamentally sciences of human relations.[1]

In emphasizing the human factor in politics, I am attacking the problem of social planning, so to speak, from the rear, i.e., not from the point of its program but from the point of view of its administration. I am emphasizing the fact that social planning is social politics, and that some of the most difficult problems it has to face are not in the field of legislation but of administration.

I might add that I am not unaware of the larger question that lies on the margin of this enquiry: the question, namely, whether there are any limits to the extent and rapidity with which changes —planned or not—can go on within the structure of an existing social and political order without destroying it. The question has been raised whether social planning, on any extensive scale, can go on within the limits of any free and secular society. Free societies, it has been asserted, grow; they are not planned.

1 James Bryce, *Modern Democracics*, 1:14; George Catlin, *The Science and Method of Politics.*

II. *Utopia*

Social planning is an ancient art, which has achieved in recent years, a new vogue. It is, in fact, as old as politics and like politics, had its origin in the city, in the *polis*, and in the problems of civilized and sophisticated existence such as the conditions of city life permit and enforce.

Social planning, of some sort, we have always had. The social worker who attempts to formulate for a client a program of social rehabilitation is in some sense engaged in social planning.

Ordinarily the task of the social agency is to meet a present and pressing emergency. But it is the experience of social agencies that a very considerable number of the cases they are called on to deal with are recurrent. This often calls for a more elaborate program, covering a longer period, and concerned with more aspects of the individual's personal and family life, and in the end, perhaps, involving the client's whole career. Frequently what was originally a personal and family problem impinges on local custom and eventually on the structure of society, and can not be adequately dealt with without some modification or reform of the existing social structure. At this point what was originally conceived to be a personal and family emergency turns out to be a social problem. This is, in fact, one of the ways in which movements for reform originate. This is typically the way social planning, on a small scale, begins.

But social problems are not wholly solved by changing the form or structure of society. It is necessary that the new social order should be understood, accepted and eventually incorporated into the habits, traditions and mores of the community. In this way it becomes a part of the routine and of the conventions of an established social order which, because it is customary and unconscious, may be said to enforce itself. Thus the social worker's task of securing the cooperation of the client in the program of his own rehabilitation is typical of the problem which arises everywhere in the effort to make social programs effective.

I might add, in parentheses, that in dealing with this very practical problem professional case workers may get some help from psychiatry but very little from psychology or sociology.

As these studies are now organized they are not designed to profit by what doctors, lawyers, newspaper men, and the police have learned about human nature, not to mention what colonial administrators have learned in their efforts at dealing with primitive and alien peoples.

Science seems to be cut off from all those sources of insight and knowledge on methodological grounds. It appears that the more scientific psychology and the social sciences have become the more they are restricted to the study of those aspects of human life that are neither characteristically human nor social.

Social planning, on a grand scale, such as has been recently undertaken in Russia and in some other European countries, has come into existence as the result of a revolution, but the task of putting the new social order into effect has involved the new societies in the same kind of problem that the social worker faces: the problem of getting the cooperation of the individual in whose habits and customs the new order, if it is established at all, must eventually take root.

The first social planners, in the grand style, were what we may describe as the Utopians. From Plato to Patrick Geddes, there has always been a Utopian strain in social thinking, which has frequently found expression in projects for the creation, somewhere, of a perfect city and an ideal state.[2]

Where these remained mere projects, and no attempt was made to set them up in a real world, they have at least made men more keenly conscious of the limitations and defects of the world in which they were living, by contrast with the spaciousness and perfection of the world of which they dreamed. In this way they have

2 With the exception, perhaps, of Aristotle's politics it was not until the publication of Machiavelli's *The Prince* that literature affords an example of a man who thought realistically and in the modern manner in the field of politics and social science, seeking to describe, not the sort of state men should desire, but rather how, human nature being what it is, such political society as existed could hope to survive in the world in which it found itself.

contributed measurably in creating a public opinion and a political power that has functioned elsewhere in some less romantic social enterprise. Social unrest and discontent with existing conditions, as practical politicians understand, is an important source of political power, provided it does not find—and sometimes when it does—expression in religious movements. Religious movements are ordinarily directed rather toward the reformation of human nature and the moral order than the economical and political structure of society.

On the other hand, when serious attempts have been made to establish these planned societies—and the number of such attempts is larger than most of us imagine—they have usually failed and the movements they inspired have been—to use communist phraseology—liquidated.

It is, however, worth noting that these Utopian enterprises lasted longer when they rested on a religious than upon economic foundations.

In this connection I might add that the ultimate success of the communist regime in Russia probably depends more upon its ability to propagate and establish a new and essentially religious faith—than upon the merits of its economic program. Meanwhile the actual central authority in this new imperium—the Federation of Soviet Republics—seems to rest in a politico-religious sect—the so-called communist party, which requires repeated and more or less regular purgings, to discipline backsliders and keep the faith pure and undefiled.

To political realists these historic Utopias to which I have referred are mere "flights from reality" which belong to the realm of poetry rather than the world of fact. To dismiss them because they are unreal and impracticable is, however, to overlook the role in collective action of what Sorel calls the "social myth."

In his volume *Reflections on Violence,* Sorel discusses candidly and acutely the function in revolutionary movements of the myth of the general strike.

"The myth," he says, "must be judged as a means of acting on the present; any attempt to discuss how far it can be taken literally as future history is devoid of sense . . . even supposing the revolutionaries to have been wholly and entirely deluded in setting up this imaginary picture of the general strike, this picture may yet have been, in the course of the preparation for the revolution, a great element of strength, if it has embraced all the aspirations of socialism, and if it has given to the whole body of revolutionary thought a precision and a rigidity which no other method of thought could have given."[3]

The Utopian myth, as he conceives it, is a social symbol rather than a social plan. Its function is, at one and the same time, to mobilize and discipline the masses by giving an "aspect of complete reality to the hopes of immediate action"—not that action is possible, but because, as he says, by this method more easily than by any other "men can reform their desires, passions and mental activity."

"Strikes," he adds a little later, "have engendered in the proletariat the noblest, deepest, and most moving sentiments they possess."[4]

III. *The Political Process*

Utopian communities have been described as attempts to solve the problems of a real world by taking refuge in a world that is visionary and unreal. But there is always likely to be a visionary and unreal element in social planning, due to the fact that social programs must be conceived and formulated, finally, in ways that are designed to capture the imagination of the people whose world they seek to improve. Otherwise they are not likely to gain the cooperation they require to be successful.

The difficulty with planned Utopias, as with more modest programs of reform, is that they seek to create a new and ideal society out of the same human elements of which the old society was composed.

Social planners have not always reckoned with human and political aspects of their problem. They have assumed that society is to such an extent an artifact that if the formal structure of exist-

3 Georges Sorel, *Reflections on Violence*, pp. 133–37.
4 Ibid.

ing institutions, and the material conditions on which the social order rests are changed, human nature and the moral order would presently respond.

There seems to be implied in the popular conception of "social lag" the notion that, in the long run, human nature always responds and eventually conforms to material conditions. No doubt it does, but sometimes it responds in ways that are neither expected nor desired.

As a matter of fact human nature and social institutions are not wholly the product of the environment, even if you define human environment as just the things to which human nature does respond. Furthermore society and the existing moral order are ordinarily so well established in tradition, custom and the personal habits of individuals that they cannot be suddenly decreed or legislated out of existence.

Once the significance of this fact is understood it emphasizes the necessity of providing in social planning a sufficiently extended period of enlightenment and education in which to make the accommodation necessarily involved in the transition from an old to a new social order.

Not only do such plans and programs need to be advertised and promoted, in order to gain acceptance, but they need, to make them effective, to be administered with some reference to and understanding of local tradition and existing customary order. The Tennessee Valley project will probably furnish, before it is completed, an instructive illustration. The whole theory of local self-government which, in spite of recent changes, still has some validity, is based on a recognition of these local differences of tradition and culture.

Originally, it would seem, local institutions came into existence and grew up quite naturally like the plants, and in that case the distinction between human nature and the existing moral order, to which John Dewey refers so feelingly in the introduction to his volume on human nature and conduct, probably did not exist.[5]

5 "Morality is largely concerned with controlling human nature. When we are attempting to control anything we are acutely aware of what resists us. So moralists were led, perhaps, to think of human nature as

It is notorious that among primitive man there is very little evidence of that intense subjective life of which more civilized and sophisticated people are often so painfully conscious.

Lord Olivier, in speaking of primitive man, referred to his life as "a full cup." By this he meant that in savage society the habits of individuals so completely conformed to what was customary and expected that the sense of human nature as something, not only different, but in conflict with the social order, did not present itself to men's minds at all.[6]

That was before the era of social planning; before the era of

---

evil because of its reluctance to yield to control, its rebelliousness under the yoke. But this explanation only raises another question. Why did morality set up rules so foreign to human nature? The ends it insisted upon, the regulations it imposed, were after all outgrowths of human nature. Why then was human nature so averse to them? . . . The fact which is forced upon us when we raise this question is the existence of classes. Control has been vested in an oligarchy. Indifference to regulation has grown in the gap which separates the ruled from the rulers. Parents, priests, chiefs, social censors have supplied aims, aims which were foreign to those upon whom they were imposed, to the young, laymen, ordinary folk; a few have given and administered rule, and the mass have in a passable fashion and with reluctance obeyed" (John Dewey, *Human Nature and Conduct*, pp. 1, 2).

6 "When a race has established and maintained itself for generations in a consistent environment—a primitive race not reaching as yet a very high degree of civilization—and has staved off the disadvantageous effects of excess of population by means of birth control, infanticide, organized emigration, or moderate chronic war with its neighbors, it will have fitted all its bodily adaptation and the processes of its daily life so fully into the mould of its natural surroundings that it will not be conscious of itself as other than a part of nature. Such a race, in the vigor of its maturity, is a full cup; its form is saturated to the skin with the energy that has forced it into the natural mould of its life; it is sensitive at the surface reacting immediately according to its own native impulse, not critical of its motives and instincts, not hesitant between feeling and action, thought and word, not sceptical where it believes. It is very fully aware of the things of its own world; it is not aware of, and does not imagine, things outside of it. The invisible, for that race, abuts entirely upon, and is concerned only with, its own visible world" (Lord Olivier, *White Capital and Colored Labor*, pp. 33, 34).

legislation and reform and of the efforts to create social institutions by reflection and by fiat.

It is probably, as Dewey suggests, not until the social engineers began to reconstruct society in accordance with some preconceived plan—not until the days of reform and revolution—that "Man's nature has been regarded with suspicion, with fear, with sour looks, sometimes with enthusiasm for its possibilities but only when these were placed in contrast with its actualities."

It is true in America as elsewhere—but probably less true here than in most other parts of the world—that local institutions have evolved slowly, and become what they are by a process of gradual adaptation. On the whole, however, as our political system had its birth in revolution so most of our social institutions have been—not planned to be sure—but produced by a continuous series of minor eruptions and reforms.

The situation has been further complicated in recent years by the multiplication of so-called pressure groups interested in promoting some single measure of reform. The result has been that innovating social legislation has been initiated through the efforts of amateur politicians, who were out of office; while the task of administering this legislation has fallen to the professionals, who were in.

This may seem a fair division of labor but the effect has been that when we speak of politics in the United States, we do not think of political policies and social programs in the Aristotelian sense, but of some unofficial organization and activity, not always understood or countenanced by the community, that is designed, perhaps, "to get out the vote" or perform some other incidental but necessary function that was not originally provided for in the plans of our democracy when it was young and new.

If these somewhat casual references to actual politics are at all convincing they will serve to suggest, at least, the place and function of social planning in the political process. The political process, as here conceived, may be said to begin at the point where formal programs and planned political action supersedes the evolutionary processes by which, in every stable society, a body of tradition and culture slowly accumulates, under the influence of which succeeding generations of men are gradually disciplined and domesticated.

The political process thus defined necessarily interrupts to some extent the customary social order and disturbs some or all of the vested interests.

Even those insidious, minor and slow-burning revolutions we call social movements—the labor movement, for example—by which old institutions are changed and new ones come into existence, if they move too rapidly and are at any time too numerous are likely to prove profoundly disturbing. For this reason the political process can only proceed in a relatively orderly way insofar as it generates a political power and authority capable of enforcing a certain degree of order and discipline until a new equilibrium has been achieved and the changes which the new programs initiated have been assimilated, digested and incorporated with the folkways of the original and historic society.

I might add that the political process, conceived in these very general terms, will operate everywhere in substantially the same fashion—in Moscow, Berlin, and Chicago—irrespective of the particular form of the government in power. This is true because every government, in order to survive and flourish, must secure eventually the consent and cooperation of the people it seeks to govern.

"It is," as the historian and philosopher Hume once said, "on opinion that government is founded; and that maxim extends to the most despotic and the most military governments as well as the most popular and free."[7]

In writing this passage Hume had in mind, no doubt, not merely that opinion which gets registered in popular elections; not merely those opinions in which men rationalize their changing responses to current events—opinions likely to be swayed by every wind of doctrine. Under opinion he included, in addition to these transient changes of mood and attitude, that body of nonrational and relatively unchanging attitudes and sentiments which

7 David Hume, *Essays*, chap. 4, "The First Principles of Government."

have grown up in the course of the history of every permanent and well-established society, and constitute an invisible, and so to speak, underground foundation which supports a superstructure of explicit and formal legislation, like the traffic regulations of which we are all the more keenly aware because we are always butting into them and getting hurt.

With respect to these foundations and this superstructure it probably is fair to say that the relative security of society can be estimated by the number of its unwritten as compared with its formal and written laws, i.e., the greater the number of laws on the statute books the less security the people who live under them are likely to enjoy.

2

REFLECTIONS ON COMMUNICATION AND CULTURE

I. *Communication in the Cultural Process*

COMMUNICATION is so obvious and pervasive a factor in social life that I have often wondered why so little had been said or written about it. Now that I have attempted to write something on the subject, I no longer wonder, I know.

One reason that there has been so little written on this subject is because there has been so much to write, and because much that has been written has been concerned with communication as it functions in some special way in some specific region of social life.

In any case, this paper has turned out to be little more than a record of my explorations and mental prospecting, seeking to define the limits of a subject of which I believed before I started that I already had some general knowledge.

There is, to be sure, an extensive literature on the subject of speech and language, including technical devices as different as the ideographs of the Stone Age and the newspaper and radio of the modern world, by which man has sought to perfect his means of communication and expand the effective limits of his world. The radio and newspaper, however, have been mere instrumental extensions of speech. Less has been written about the manifold types of symbolism, including the so-called fine arts, by which sentiments and attitudes as well as ideas are communicated.

There is also an extensive psychological and sociological literature which approaches the subject of communication obliquely

---

Reprinted from the *American Journal of Sociology* 44 (September 1938): 187–205.

and from the point of view of some ulterior interest. In the writings of the Scottish moral philosophers, from Bishop Butler to Hume and Adam Smith, one notes an insistent reference to the facts of sympathy and of imitation as offering at once an evidence and an explanation of that understanding and solidarity which is the basis of the moral order. A little later, in 1872, Walter Bagehot, in a volume, *Physics and Politics*, which has become a sociological classic, emphasizes the importance of imitation and indicates its role in the cultural process and in social life. Eighteen years later when Gabriel Tarde published his *Laws of Imitation*, he identified imitation, which he described as "action of one mind upon another at a distance," with the fundamental social and cultural process. The forms in which communication takes place are obviously protean. They include not merely sympathy and imitation, which are generally recognized as such in the literature of the subject, but discussion, dialectic, and suggestion.

The nature and function of communication appears in a new light in the studies of personality and self-consciousness and in the writings of men as widely divergent in their several points of view as J. Mark Baldwin, Charles H. Cooley, and George H. Mead. Communication and the nature of the process by which one mind knows another turns up again as a cardinal problem of the so-called "understanding sociology" (*verstehende Soziologie*) of Max Weber and in the writings of Wilhelm Dilthey, who preceded and influenced him.

Finally there are the semanticists, of whom C. K. Ogden and I. A. Richards, authors of *The Meaning of Meaning*, seem to be the most eminent representatives. They are interested not primarily in communication but in intelligibility, which as far as I am concerned, they have not always achieved. And finally as I write these words, I note the appearance of a new volume by Stuart Chase, *The Tyranny of Words*, in which he undertakes to tell us in simple language what Ogden and Richards meant when they wrote *The Meaning of Meaning*.

Implicit in all this discussion—and that, it seems to me, is the important thing—is the notion that communication is a form of interaction or a process that takes place between persons—that is to say, individuals with an ego, individuals with a point of view, conscious of themselves and more or less oriented in a moral world. Communication is, therefore, not a form of interstimulation merely. The term would not properly apply to two individuals who by occupying the same bed kept one another warm. Communication when completed involves an interpretation by *A* of the stimulus coming from *B*, and a reference of that interpretation back to the person of whose sentiment or attitude it assumes to be an expression.

Let me illustrate. If innocently, as is my wont, I am walking along the street and a brick falls on my head or close enough at least to interrupt my meditations, that in itself is a mere physical fact. If, however, looking up I see a face grinning down on me maliciously from the wall from which the brick came, the fall of that brick ceases to be a mere physical phenomenon and becomes a social fact. It changes its character as soon as I interpret it as an expression of attitude or intent rather than an act of God—that being the secular language in which we describe a happening that is wholly without intention of any sort, and one, therefore, for which no one can be made responsible.

Communication is then a form of interaction that takes place, typically at least, between individuals with an ego. I am leaving out of the reckoning, for the present, the kind and quality of the communication which obviously takes place among less articulate creatures than ourselves.

You have no doubt observed the ceremonious way in which two strange dogs approach each other. This is not mere interstimulation; it is communication. These dogs understand one another, even when they do not speak. So it is with the hen clucking to her chicks. This is not conversation, but it is communication. What the natural history of the process is I shall not undertake to discuss. The origin of languages is one of the classic problems of the students of linguistics. The case of hen and chicks was one of the favorite themes of George Mead's lectures on social psychology.

The most interesting thing I have been able to find in the books on the subject of communication is Edward Sapir's article on "Language" in the *Encyclopedia of the Social Sciences;* that, and two briefer articles by the same author, one on "Communication" and the other on "Symbolism." Sapir, following in this Ogden and Richards, distinguishes between language that is symbolic and impersonal—like a mathematical formula or the number system—and language that is expressive and personal, like a gesture or an expletive, or even a voice crying in the wilderness. In the first case the function of language is purely "referential," as in scientific discourse. It points out its object, identifies, classifies, and describes it. In the second case, language, modulated by accent, intonation, and inflection, tends to be expressive merely. In that case the function of words seems to be to reveal the mood and the sentiments of the person who utters them, rather than to define and express an idea.

The same distinction applies, in varying degrees, to forms of communication as different as the sign language used by deaf-mutes and what I may call the "expressive arts," particularly music and dancing. In every form which the process of communication assumes and in all the variations involved due to the different means employed, the distinction between the referential or didactic function—where ideas are communicated—and the expressive function—where sentiments and attitudes are manifested—persists. In the one case ideas, and in the other sentiments, attitudes, and emotions are communicated, partly through the medium of conventional symbols and partly through gesture and expressive behavior, by which I mean behavior that can be interpreted intuitively. Music and dancing are expressions of this sort. They seem to be expressions of what Schopenhauer calls pure will. In the same sense mathematics and logic may be described as expressions of pure form or idea.

To pursue these divergent lines of inquiry farther, however, would lead into a discussion of the manner in which logic and science on the one hand, and the expressive arts on the other, have developed out of the impulse and the efforts of human beings to communicate their ideas and express their sentiments. My purpose is rather to emphasize the fact that communication as I understand it is, if not identical with, at least indispensable to, the cultural process. Culture may assume among different peoples at different times and places many and varied forms, material and non-material—language, marriage customs, and artifacts, like the hoe and the plow, all alike are cultural traits. It is, however, the fact that they are understood by a particular people, by a cultural group, that gives them the character we describe as cultural. Culture includes then all that is communicable; and its fundamental components, whatever the forms and symbols in which they may be anywhere embodied, are, in the sense in which Schopenhauer seems to have used those terms, Will and Idea. Attitudes and sentiments, folkways and mores, are the warp and woof of that web of understanding we call "culture." I follow Sapir in the assumption that the essence of culture is understanding.

II. *Communication and Competition*

What does communication do and how does it function in the cultural process? It seems to do several different things. Communication creates, or makes possible at least, that consensus and understanding among the individual components of a social group which eventually gives it and them the character not merely of society but of a cultural unit. It spins a web of custom and mutual expectation which binds together social entities as diverse as the family group, a labor organization, or the haggling participants in a village market. Communication maintains the concert necessary to enable them to function, each in its several ways.

Family group or labor organization, every form of society except the most transient has a life-history and a tradition. It is by communication that this tradition is transmitted. It is in this way that the continuity of common enterprises and social institutions is maintained, not merely from day to day, but from generation to generation. Thus the function of communication seems to be to maintain the unity and integrity of the social group in its two dimensions—space and time. It is in recognition of this fact that John Dewey has said: "Society not only continues to exist by transmission, by communication, but may fairly be said to exist in transmission, in communication."

Implicit in Dewey's statement, however, is a conception of

society that is not generally nor everywhere accepted, since it seems to identify the social with the moral order. By so doing it limits the term "social" to those relations of individuals that are personal, customary, and moral.

When individuals use one another to get results, without reference to their emotional or intellectual disposition and consent, says Dewey, they are involved in relations that are not social. To make the matter clear, he adds, "So far as the relations of parent and child, teacher and pupil remain upon this level, they form no true social group, no matter how closely their respective activities touch one another."

It is obvious, however, that communication, if it is the typical social process, is not the only form of interaction that goes on among the individual units of a social group. "We are compelled to recognize," he admits, "that even within the most social group there are many relations which are not yet social"—not social, at any rate, in the sense in which he uses the term. Competition, for example, performs a social function of a somewhat different sort, but one that is at least comparable to that of communication. The economic order in society seems to be very largely a by-product of competition. In any case, competition is, as Cooley observes, "the very heart of the economic process." What we ordinarily designate as economic competition, however, is not competition in the Malthusian sense of that term in which it is identical with the struggle for existence. Economic competition is always competition that is controlled and regulated to some extent by convention, understanding, and law.

The investigations of plant and animal ecologists have discovered that even where competition is free and unrestricted, as it is in the so-called plant and animal communities, there exists among creatures living in the same habitat a kind of natural economy. What characterizes this economy is a division of labor and an unconscious cooperation of competing organisms. Wherever in nature competition or the struggle for existence brings about a stable organization among competing individuals, it is because they have achieved in some form or another a division of labor and some form of conscious or unconscious cooperation. In such case the competing species or individual, each occupying the particular niche in which it fits, will have created an environment in which all can live together under conditions where each could not live separately. This natural economy of plants and animals is called symbiosis.

Man's relation to other men is, to a very much larger extent than has hitherto been recognized, symbiotic rather than social, in the sense in which Dewey uses that term. Competition among plants and animals tends to bring about an orderly distribution as well as a mutual adaptation of the species living together in a common habitat. Competition among human beings has brought about, or at any rate helped to bring about, not merely a territorial, but an occupational distribution of races and peoples. Incidentally, it has brought about that inevitable division of labor which is fundamental to every permanent form of society from the family to the nation.

If the struggle for existence, as Darwin conceived it, was a determining factor in producing that diversity of living types described in the *Origin of the Species*, then economic competition, the struggle for a livelihood, seems to have been a decisive factor in bringing about among human beings a comparable occupational diversity. But this division of labor wherever it exists in human society is limited by custom; and custom is a product of communication.

As a matter of fact, competition and communication operate everywhere within the same local habitat and within the same community, but in relative independence of each other. The area of competition and of the symbiotic relationship is, however, invariably wider and more inclusive than the area of those intimate, personal, and moral relations initiated by communication. Commerce invariably expands more widely and rapidly than linguistic or cultural understanding. It is, it seems, this cultural lag that makes most of our political and cultural problems. But the main point is that communication, where it exists, invariably modifies and qualifies competition, and the cultural order imposes limitations on the symbiotic.

Most of you will perhaps recall Sumner's description of primitive society, a territory occupied by little scattered ethnocentric groups, each the focus and center of a little world in which all members are bound together in ties of mutual understanding and loyalty.

Outside of these little tribal and familial units, on the other hand, men live in relation with one another not unlike those in which they live with the plants and animals, that is to say, in a kind of symbiosis, very little modified by mutual understanding or agreements of any sort. Under these circumstances the fundamental social and economic order is enforced and maintained by competition, but competition modified and controlled to an ever-increasing degree by custom, convention, and law.

As a matter of fact, society everywhere exhibits two fundamental forms of organization—the familial and the communal. Familial society seems to have had its source in the interest and in the urge of individuals, not merely to live as individuals but to perpetuate the race. Thus the family seems to rest, finally, on an instinctive basis. Communal society, on the other hand, has arisen out of the need of the individuals to survive as individuals. Under these conditions men have come together, not in response to some gregarious impulse comparable with the sexual instinct, but for the more pragmatic and intelligible reason that they are useful to one another.

In spite of the changes which time and civilization have wrought in the existing social order, man lives as he always has, in two worlds—the little world of the family and the great world of commerce and politics. In the little world the order which predominates is intimate, personal, and moral. In the larger world man is free to pursue his individual interests in his own individual way, relatively uninhibited by the expectations and claims which, in a more intimate social order, the interests of others might impose upon him. In the family it is communication and the personal influences which communication mediates that are the source and principle of order. In the world of commerce, and to a less degree in politics, it is competition, and competition in the more sublimated form of conflict and rivalry, which imposes such order as exists.

What all this suggests, though not perhaps so obviously as I should like, is that competition and communication, although they perform divergent and uncoordinated social functions, nevertheless in the actual life of society supplement and complete each other.

Competition seems to be the principle of individuation in the life of the person and of society. Under the influence of this principle the individual adapts and accommodates himself, not merely to the human habitat but to the occupational organization of the society of which he is a member. He follows the vocation and does the thing he can, rather than the thing he might like to do. Communication, on the other hand, operates primarily as an integrating and socializing principle.

It is true, of course, that when new forms of communication have brought about more intimate associations among individuals or peoples who have been culturally isolated, the first consequence may be to intensify competition. Furthermore, under the influence of communication, competition tends to assume a new character. It becomes conflict. In that case the struggle for existence is likely to be intensified by fears, animosities, and jealousies, which the presense of the competitor and the knowledge of his purposes arouse. Under such circumstances a competitor becomes an enemy.

On the other hand, it is always possible to come to terms with an enemy whom one knows and with whom one can communicate, and, in the long run, greater intimacy inevitably brings with it a more profound understanding, the result of which is to humanize social relations and to substitute a moral order for one that is fundamentally symbiotic rather than social, always in the restricted sense of that term.

III. *Diffusion*

Communication, whether it takes place through the medium of gesture, articulate speech, or conventional symbols of any sort whatever, always involves, it seems to me, an interpretation of the attitude or intent of the person whose word or gesture supplied the stimulus. What anything means to anyone at any time is substantially what it means, has meant, or will mean, to someone else. Communication is a process or form of interaction that is interpersonal, i.e., social in the narrower sense. The process is complete only when it results in some sort of understanding. In other words, communication is never merely a case of stimulus and response in the sense in which those terms are used in individual psychology. It is rather expression, interpretation, and response.

In some cases, in most cases perhaps, and particularly where the persons involved are *en rapport*, the response of individual *A* to an expressive action of individual *B* is likely to be immediate and well-nigh automatic. This is obviously so in the case of hypnotic suggestion, and particularly so under the condition of what is called "isolated rapport," where the subject responds to the suggestions of the hypnotizer and to those of no one else.

We must conceive individuals in society as living constantly enveloped in an atmosphere of subconscious suggestion. In this atmosphere they are constantly responsive, not merely to the overt acts but to the moods and the presence of other persons, in somewhat the same way that they are to the weather. What we call the fluctuations of public opinion, public sentiment, and fashion, are, in fact, a kind of social weather. These changes in the social weather evoke changes in internal tensions of persons who are *en rapport:* changes so subtle that they amount to a kind of clairvoyance. It is only in moments of abstraction that this condition of clairvoyance is interrupted and then only partially. A suggestion is, of course, not a mere stimulus, but a stimulus that is interpreted as an expression of a wish or an attitude. The literature of hypnotism indicates how subtle suggestions may be and how responsive under certain conditions individuals may be to them.

Sometimes, to be sure, the sense and meaning of the behavior and language of those about us are obscure; this sets us thinking, and leaves us sometimes with a sense of frustration and confusion. At other times it arouses us, not to definite action, but to vague emotional protest or inarticulate opposition. This emotional expression of unrest, multiplied and intensified by the reflex influence of mind on mind, may take the form finally of a social brainstorm like the dancing mania of the Middle Ages or the commercial panic of 1929. Under more normal conditions unrest may express itself in social agitation or in the less violent form of discussion and debate.

These are some of the manifold ways in which communication operating within the limits of an existing culture group changes, directly and indirectly, the pattern of cultural life. If I merely refer to these manifestations here in passing it is because a fuller discussion of them would involve problems of collective behavior which are so diverse and manifold that they have become the subject of a special discipline of the social sciences.

The cultural process ordinarily presents itself in two dimensions or aspects which are intimately bound up with and determined by the condition under which communication inevitably takes place. They are: diffusion and acculturation.

As communication takes place between persons, it is necessarily involved in all the complexities incident to the transmission of a stimulus from the source *a quo* to a terminus *ad quem*—i.e., from a person of whose mind it is an expression to the person in whose mind it finds a response. The obvious conditions which facilitate or obstruct these processes are mainly physical and in modern times they have been progressively overcome by means of technical devices like the alphabet, printing press, radio, etc.

The less obvious obstacles to effective communication are the difficulties that grow out of differences of language, tradition, experience, and interest. By interest in this instance I mean what Thomas refers to as the "run of attention." Everywhere and always, certain interests, persons, or events are in the focus of attention; certain things are in fashion. Whatever has importance and prestige at the moment has power to direct for a time the currents of public opinion, even if it does not change, in the long run, the trend of events. All these things are factors in communication and either facilitate or make difficult the transmission of news from one country to another. The manner in which news circulates is typical of one way in which cultural diffusion takes place.

Discussions of the deficiencies of the press often proceed on the implicit assumption that the communication of news from one cultural area to another—from the Orient to the Occident, for example, or from Berlin to New York—is an operation as simple as the transportation of a commodity like bricks. One can, of course, transport words across cultural marches, but the interpretations which they receive on two sides of a political or cultural boundary will depend upon the context which their different interpreters bring to them. That context, in turn, will depend rather more upon the past experience and present temper of the people to whom the words are addressed than upon either the art or the good will of the persons who report them.

Foreign correspondents know, as no one who has not had the experience, how difficult it is under ordinary circumstances to make the public read foreign news. They know, also, how much more difficult it is to make events happening beyond his horizon intelligible to the average man in the street. In general, news circulates widely in every direction in proportion as it is interesting and intelligible. In that respect it is not unlike any other cultural item, the oil cans of the Standard Oil Company or the Singer sewing machine for example, which are now possibly the most widely dispersed of all our modern cultural artifacts.

Each and every artifact or item of news inevitably tends to reach finally the places where it will be appreciated and understood. Cultural traits are assimilated only as they are understood, and they are understood only as they are assimilated. This does not mean that a cultural artifact or an item of news will have everywhere the same meaning; quite the contrary. But the different meanings they do have in different places will tend to converge, as diffusion is succeeded by acculturation.

It is extraordinary to what extent and with what rapidity news tends to reach the minds of those to whom its message, if intelligible, is important. On the other hand, just as important, if less remarkable, is the difficulty of communicating a message that is neither important nor intelligible to the persons to whom it is addressed. This latter is a problem of the schools, particularly the problem of rote learning.

Thirty-three years ago the conclusion of the Russian-Japanese War made news that I suspect circulated farther and more rapidly than any other report of events had ever traveled before. One heard echoes of it in regions as far apart as the mountain fastnesses of Tibet and the forests of Central Africa. It was the news that a nation of colored people had defeated and conquered a nation of white people. The same item of news might travel farther and with greater speed today, but it would not have the same importance. The question of how and why and under what circumstances news circulates is an important one and deserves more attention than has yet been given to it.

It is a familiar observation of students of the cultural process that artifacts, the traits of a material culture, are more easily diffused and more rapidly assimilated than similar items of a nonmaterial culture—political institutions and religious practices, for example. That is no more than to say that trade expands, on the whole, more rapidly than religion. But that, too, depends upon circumstances. Consider, for example, the sudden rapid diffusion in the modern world of communism.

One reason the terms of a material culture are so widely diffused and easily assimilated is because their uses are obvious and their values, whatever they be, are rational and secular. One needs no rite or ceremony to initiate him into mysteries involved in the use of a wheelbarrow or rifle. When the first plow was introduced into South Africa, an old chief who was invited to be present and see the demonstration recognized its value at once. He said, "This is a great thing the white man has brought us." Then after some reflection he added: "It is worth as much as ten wives."

What we call civilization, as distinguished from culture, is largely composed of such artifacts and technical devices as can be diffused without undermining the existing social institutions and without impairing the ability of a people to act collectively, that is to say, consistently and in concert. Institutions seem to exist primarily to facilitate collective action, and anything that involves a society rather than the individuals of which that society is composed is hard to export. Diffusion takes place more easily when the social unity is relaxed.

It is no secret, I suppose, that there is inevitably an intimate and indissoluble relation between commerce and the news. The centers of trade are invariably the centers of news; the centers to which the news inevitably comes and from whence it is diffused, first to the local community and then, according to its interests and importance, to the ends of the earth.

During this diffusion a process of selection necessarily takes place. Some news items travel farther and more rapidly than others. This is true even when all or most of the physical obstacles to communication have been overcome. The reason of course is simple enough. It is bound up with the inevitably egocentric character of human beings and the ethnocentric character of human relations generally. An event is important only as we believe we can do something about it. It loses importance in proportion as the possibility of doing that something seems more remote. An earthquake in China assumes, in view of our incorrigible provincialism, less importance than a funeral in our village. This is an example of what is meant by social distance, which sociologists seek to conceptualize and, in some sense, [use to] measure personal relations and personal intimacies. Importance is ultimately a personal matter; a matter of social distance.

The principle involved in the circulation of news is not different from that involved in the cultural process of diffusion, wherever it takes place. Individuals and societies assimilate most readily, as I have said, what is at once interesting and intelligible.

IV. *Acculturation*

If the marketplace is the center from which news is disseminated and cultural influences are diffused, it is, likewise, the center in which old ideas go into the crucible and new ideas emerge. The marketplace where men gather to dicker and chaffer, is in the very nature of things a kind of forum where men of diverse interests and different minds are engaged in peaceful controversy, trying to come to terms about values and prices; trying, also, by a process that is fundamentally dialectical, to explore the different meanings things have for men of different interests; seeking to reach understandings based rather more on reason and rather less on tradition and the prejudices which custom has sanctioned, if not sanctified. It is for this reason that the great metropolitan cities—Rome, London, and Paris—cities to which peoples come and go from the four ends of the earth, are in a perpetual ferment of enlightenment, are continually involved, to use a German expression, in an *Aufklärung*. Under such conditions the historical process is quickened, and acculturation, the mutual interpenetration of minds and cultures, goes forward at a rapid pace.

When peoples of different races and divergent cultures seek to live together within the limits of the same local economy, they are likely to live for a time in relations which I have described as symbiotic rather than social, using that term in this connection as Dewey and others have used it, namely, as identical with cultural. They live, in short, in physical contiguity, but in more or less complete moral isolation, a situation which corresponds in effect if not in fact, to Sumner's description of primitive society.

This has been and still is the situation of some of those little religious sects like the Mennonites, which have from time to time sought refuge in the United States and elsewhere, settling on the frontiers of European civilization, where they might hope to live in something like tribal isolation—untrammeled and uncorrupted by intercourse with a gentile world.

It was to preserve this isolation that some of Pennsylvania's "plain people," the Amish, protested a few months ago against a gift of $112,000 of P.W.A. funds which the government was pressing upon them for new schoolhouses. New schools, in this case, involved the use of busses, to which the "plain people" were opposed. They believed, also, and no doubt quite correctly, that intimate association of Amish children with the mixed population of a consolidated school to whom Amish folkways would certainly seem quaint would undermine the discipline and the sacred solidarity of the Amish society.

This situation, in which peoples occupying the same territory live in a moral isolation more or less complete, was historically, so long as they lived in the seclusion of their religious community, the situation of a more sophisticated people than the Amish, namely, the Jews. It has been, to a less extent, the situation of every immigrant people which has for any reason sought to find a place in the economic order of an established society and at the same time maintain a cultural tradition that was alien to it.

Inevitably, however, in the natural course, under modern conditions of life, both the immigrant and the sectarian seek to escape from this isolation in order that they may participate more actively in the social life of the people about them. It is then, if not earlier, that they become aware of the social distance that sets them apart from the members of the dominant cultural group. Under these circumstances acculturation becomes involved in and part of the struggle of immigrants and sectarians alike for status. Everything that marks them as strangers—manners, accent, habits of speech and thought—makes this struggle difficult. The cultural conflict which then ensues—whether openly manifested or merely sensed —tends, as conflict invariably does, to heighten self-consciousness in members of both cultural groups, in those who are classed as aliens and in those who count themselves native.

However, anything that intensifies self-consciousness and stimulates introspection inevitably brings to the surface and into clear consciousness sentiments and attitudes that otherwise would escape rational criticism and interpretation. Otherwise they would probably, as the psychoanalysts tell us, continue active in the dark backgrounds of consciousness. They would still function as part of that "vital secret" to which William James refers in his essay *A Certain Blindness in Human Beings*—a secret of which each of us is profoundly conscious because it is the substance of one's own self-consciousness and of one's individual point of view—but for which we look in vain to others for sympathy and understanding. But conflict, and particularly cultural conflict, in so far as it brings into the light of understanding impulses and attitudes of which we would otherwise remain unconscious, inevitably increases our knowledge not merely of ourselves but of our fellows, since the attitudes and sentiments which we find in ourselves we are able to appreciate and understand, no matter how indirectly expressed, when we find them in the minds of others.

Acculturation if we conceive it in radical fashion, may be said to begin with the intimate associations and understandings that grow up in the family between mother and child and somewhat later with other members of the family. But while mothers are necessarily, and under all ordinary circumstances, profoundly interested and responsive to their children, it is notorious that they do not always understand them.

The situation differs, but not greatly, with other members of the family—notably with the relations between husband and wife. Men are naturally and instinctively interested in and attracted by women, particularly strange women, but they often find them difficult to understand. In fact men have felt in the past and still feel in some obscure way, I suspect, that women, no matter how interesting, are not quite human in the sense and to the degree that this is true of themselves.

If this is not true to the same extent today that it once was, it is because men and women, in the family and outside of it, live in more intimate association with one another than they formerly did. They still have their separate worlds, but they get together as they formerly did not. They speak the same language. But this is true also of parents and children. Both understand each other better than they once did.

Men and women have learned a great deal about one another from experience, but they have learned more—in the sense of understanding one another and in the ability to communicate—from literature and the arts. In fact it is just the function of literature and the arts and of what are described in academic circles as the humanities to give us this intimate personal and inside knowledge of each other which makes social life more amiable and collective action possible.

I am, perhaps, wrong in describing the intimate associations which family life permits and enforces as if they were part and parcel of the cultural process. That may seem to be employing a term in a context which is so foreign to it as to destroy its original meaning. I am not sure, however, that this is quite true. At any rate, in the family in which husband and wife are of different racial stocks, with different cultural heritages, the process of acculturation—and acculturation in the sense in which it is familiar to students—takes place more obviously and more effectively than it does elsewhere. It is this fact and not its biological consequences which gives recent studies of race mixture and interracial marriage, like the studies of Romanzo Adams in Hawaii, a significance they would not otherwise have. It is in the life histories of mixed bloods whose origin ordinarily imposes upon them the task of assimilating the heritages of two divergent cultures, that the process and consequences of acculturation are most obvious and open to investigation. The reason is that the man of mixed blood is a "marginal man," so called, that is, the man who lives in two worlds but is not quite at home in either.

In discussing cultural diffusion I have taken news and its circulation as an illustration of the process of diffusion. In doing so I have had in mind the wide distribution of news that has taken place with the extension of the means of communication through the medium of the printing press, telegraphy, and the radio. I should add, perhaps, that not everything printed in the newspaper is news. Much that is printed as news is read, at least, as if it were literature; read, that is to say, because it is thrilling and stirs the imagination and not because its message is urgent and demands action. Such, for example, are the "human interest" stories, so called, which have been so influential in expanding and maintaining newspaper circulation. But human interest stories are not news. They are literature. Time and place are the essence of news, but time and place impose no limitations on the circulation of literature and art. It is art and literature, and particularly the art of the moving picture rather than the newspaper which exercise, I suspect, the most profound and subversive cultural influences in the world today.

If the newspaper and the circulation of news seem to be the most obvious illustration of diffusion, the cinema and the motion picture seem to be the most obvious example of acculturation. The cinema deals with themes that are closer to the interests and the understanding of the ordinary man than are those of the newspaper. Besides, news is very largely concerned with business and politics, and the ordinary man, as Mr. Mencken and other newspaper men have discovered, is not profoundly interested in either.

Furthermore, the moving picture touches and enlivens men on a lower level of culture than it is possible to do through the medium of the printed page.

I have observed Negro audiences in some of the remote islands of the West Indies, where the level of literacy is very low, convulsed with laughter and mad with delight in watching the antics of Fatty Arbuckle; and I have seen the startled, cynical laughter of native audiences in the Pedang Highlands in Sumatra witnessing for the first time some of the, to them, incredibly intimate scenes of a Hollywood wooing. Anyone who has had an opportunity to observe the influence of the moving picture in any of the outlying regions of the world and upon peoples to whom its vivid transcripts of contemporary American life have come as a sudden and astonishing revelation, can have no doubt about the profound and revolutionary changes they have already wrought in the attitudes and cultures of peoples, even in the most remote parts of the world.

It is not possible, on the basis of my limited observation, to determine whether the influence of the newspaper, the cinema, or the radio has been more effective in the cultural process or more decisive in bringing about cultural changes. The influence of each has at least been different.

In conclusion, I shall revert to the distinction with which I started—the distinction between language and forms of communication which are referential, as in scientific description, and language and forms of communication which are symbolic and expressive, as in literature and the fine arts. It seems clear that the function of news is definitely referential. If it does not have the status in science of a classified fact, it is at least indispensable to government and to business. On the other hand, the function of art and of the cinema is, on the whole, in spite of the use that has been made of it for educational purposes, definitely symbolic, and as such it profoundly influences sentiment and attitudes even when it does not make any real contribution to knowledge.

3

SYMBIOSIS AND SOCIALIZATION: A FRAME OF REFERENCE FOR THE STUDY OF SOCIETY

I. *Human Society and Human Ecology*

HUMAN society everywhere presents itself to the disinterested observer in many, but particularly in two, divergent aspects. Society is obviously a collection of individuals living together, like plants and animals within the limits of a common habitat, and it is, of course, something more. It is, though perhaps not always, a collection of individuals capable of some sort of concerted and consistent action.

Viewed abstractly, as it appears, perhaps, to the geographer or to the demographer, who scrutinizes it with reference to numbers, density, and distribution of the individual units of which it is made up, any society may seem no more than an agglomeration of discrete individuals, no one of which is visibly related to, or dependent upon, any other.

Closer observation of this seemingly uncoordinated aggregate is likely to disclose a more or less typical order and pattern in the territorial distribution of its component units. Furthermore, as numbers increase this pattern is likely to exhibit a typical succession of changes. Such a settled and territorially organized society is ordinarily described as a community.

A more searching inquiry is likely to reveal the fact that this particular society, and others of the same type, so far from being, as the demographer might be disposed to conceive them, mere aggregates of statistical entities, are better described as constellations of interacting individuals, each individual unit strategically

---

Reprinted from the *American Journal of Sociology* 45 (1939): 1–25.

located with reference to its dependence upon every other, as well as upon the common habitat. One further item: the whole constellation will be in a state of more or less unstable equilibrium.

This condition of unstable equilibrium permits a community to preserve at once its functional unity and continuity—i.e., its identity in time and space—by the constant redistribution of its population with relatively minor readjustments of the functional relations of its individual units. In such a community the existing territorial order, as well as the functional relations of the individuals and of the groups of which the population is composed, will be measurably controlled by competition or, to use a more inclusive term, by what Darwin described as the "struggle for existence."

This, in brief and in substance, is the conception of human society as it appears from the point of view of human ecology. The main point is that the community so conceived is at once a territorial and a functional unit.

Described in this fashion, abstractly, and without reference to its other and more concrete characteristics, the human is not essentially different from the plant community. I should like to add, if the comment were not wholly irrelevant, that it is a comfort in these days of turmoil and strife to realize that society and human beings, when in repose, do retain and exhibit some of the dignity and serenity of plants.

There is another point of view from which one may look at society—a point of view from which it does not appear as a community, not at least as a mere agglomeration of relatively fixed and settled units, but as an association of individuals participating in a collective act. The most obvious illustration of such a unit, the family, preserves its identity and integrity not merely when it is settled but when it migrates. Communities can hardly be said to migrate. Other examples of collective entities that act are mobs, gangs, political parties, pressure groups, classes, castes, nationalities, and nations. Anything that migrates in mass—a swarm of bees, a pack of wolves, or a herd of cattle—is likely to exhibit some or all of the characteristics of such societies as are capable of collective action.

It seems that every possible form of association is or should be capable, under certain circumstances, of collective action. But there are types of communities, the individual members of which live in a condition of interdependence that is sometimes described as social, which are, nevertheless, quite incapable of collective action. With the extension of commercial intercourse to every natural region of the earth one may perhaps say that the whole world is living in a kind of symbiosis; but the world community is at present, at least, quite incapable of collective action.

Symbiosis is ordinarily defined as the living together of distinct and dissimilar species, especially when the relationship is mutually beneficial.[1] But Wheeler, in his notable volume on the social insects, says that social life—all social life—"may, indeed, be regarded merely as a special form of symbiosis."[2] Other writers would, perhaps, be disposed to regard every form of symbiotic relationship as in some sense and to some degree social. At any rate there are many forms of human association in which there is cooperation sufficient to maintain a common economy, but no communication and no consensus sufficient to insure anything like effective collective action.[3] Any association in which widely scattered individuals unconsciously compete and cooperate, or by exchange of goods and services constitute themselves an economic unit, may be described as an entity that is symbiotic rather than social; that is, in the restricted sense in which the term is used when we think of the family as the prototype of every other species of social group.

But there are forms of association in which human beings live upon society as predators or parasites upon a host; or they live together in a relation in which they perform, directly or indirectly, some obscure function of mutual benefit but of which neither they nor their symbionts are conscious. All these varied forms of associ-

1 See *An Ecological Glossary* (Norman, Okla.: University of Oklahoma Press, 1938), p. 268.

2 William Morton Wheeler, *Social Life among the Insects* (New York: Harcourt, Brace & Co., 1923), p. 195.

3 Robert E. Park, "Reflections on Communication and Culture," *American Journal of Sociology*, September 1938, p. 192.

ation may be described as examples of symbiosis, but they are forms of association that are not social in the sense in which that term is ordinarily applied to human relations, particularly such relations as are recognized by the custom and enforced by the expectation of the "customers."

One remembers the so-called "silent trade," of which we have some infrequent accounts in the history of European contacts with primitive peoples. Here there is contact—some sort of understanding but no custom. Was this form of association symbiotic or social? This is clearly a marginal case.[4] And then there are in India the "criminal tribes" and pariah peoples who live in a kind of symbiotic relation with other peoples of that country. And there are finally the occupational castes, where individuals and groups of individuals live and work together under the terms of some general understanding but do not eat together or marry. Castes are not species and they do, in spite of regulations forbidding it, interbreed. However, caste relations may be regarded in some sense as symbiotic, since they bring peoples together in economic and industrial relations while they prohibit the intimacies and understandings which seem necessary to participation in a single moral order—such an order as one expects to find in a society democratically organized.

It is quite possible for castes to live together, each performing a distinct function in the economy of which it is a part. But it is likely to be difficult, though not impossible, for castes to participate in a collective act, such as is involved in the formation of a national state. The government of India is likely, when and if it achieves its independence of England, to retain its imperial character, since it will continue to be a collection of ethnic and linguistic minorities. Nationalism and imperialism, also, for that matter, invariably assume the existence of a kind of solidarity which is ordinarily created in the process of acting collectively, but which involves active participation of all individual units in the common purpose.

There are, of course, a great many kinds of collective action; the most elementary and the most pervasive is undoubtedly mass

4 P. J. Hamilton Grierson, *The Silent Trade* (Edinburgh, 1903).

migration. Bees swarm, birds migrate, and human beings rush madly hither and yon in search for some new El Dorado or in hope of achieving somewhere a new Utopia. Collective action of every sort requires some form of communication; only in this way is it possible to achieve and maintain a concert and a consistency in the movements of individual units that we ordinarily ascribe to an act, in contrast with the casual and undirected movements in which mere impulse finds expression.[5]

It is apparent that we are concerned here with different types of association brought about and maintained, in the main and on the whole, one by competition and the other by communication, or both. The one is symbiotic and takes the form, ordinarily, of a division of labor among competing organisms or groups of organisms. The other is social in the ordinary and more restricted use of that term and is based on communication and consensus, which implies a kind of solidarity based on participation in a common enterprise and involving the more or less complete subordination of individuals to the intent and purpose of the group as a whole.

The way in which competition and communication function, the one to bring about the further specialization and individuation of the individual and the other to bring about the integration and subordination of individuals to the interests of society, I have indicated in the paper on "Communication," cited above. What remains to be made clear is how these two types of organization, the symbiotic and the social, interact and combine to bring about the specific types of association—ecological, economic, political, or customary and cultural—which distinguish the institutions of society or the types of social organizations which constitute the subject matter of the several social sciences, ecology, economics, politics, and sociology.

Sociology, as ordinarily conceived, is primarily concerned with the nature and natural history of institutions, with the processes by which institutions develop and eventually evolve the specific and stable forms in which we know them. But customary cultural and

5 Walter Heape et al., *Emigration, Migration and Nomadism* (Cambridge: W. Heffer & Sons, Ltd., 1931), pp. 137–46; Charles Elton, *Animal Ecology* (New York: Macmillan Co., 1927), pp. 132–33.

moral relations are notoriously dependent on, and responsive to, political, economic, and, ultimately, those more elementary associations brought about by the sheer struggle for existence. And besides that, the more intimate and familial types of association grow up within an environment created by the freer, more individualistic, and secular association of a political and economic society.

II. *Institutions and Collective Behavior*

Institutions have their setting in actual interests and affairs of ordinary life and sometimes arise quite suddenly in response to the pressure of some necessity—a flood, a famine, a war—anything which makes collective action urgent. This is, at any rate, the way in which fascist institutions have arisen in Italy and Germany. Labor organizations, for example, came into existence in order to carry on strikes and to direct the slow-burning revolution which is gradually transforming the capitalist system. Courts of arbitration have arisen in the same way in order to deal with the conflicts of capital and labor in situations where, because of the existence of a constitutional struggle, administrative law could not be effectively applied in dealing with the situation.

Not every social movement terminates in a new institution, but the necessity of carrying on programs initiated in some social emergency has been responsible for many if not most modern and recent institutions. Nor is it always possible to determine precisely the point at which a social movement merges into an institution. The ladies of the Y.W.C.A. used to say that theirs was not an institution but a movement. This was intended, perhaps, to disinguish it from the Y.M.C.A. which presumably had been a movement but had become an institution. Every social movement may, however, be described as a potential institution. And every institution may in turn be described as a movement that was once active and eruptive, like a volcano, but has since settled down to something like routine activity. It has, to change the metaphor, defined its aims, found its place and function in the social complex, achieved an organization, and, presumably, provided itself with a corps of functionaries to carry on its program. It becomes an institution finally when the community and the public it seeks to serve accept it, know what to expect of it, and adjust to it as a going concern. An institution may be regarded as finally established when the community and the public in which and for which it exists claim as a right the services to which they have become accustomed.

Other institutions arise more slowly and less obviously. Coming into existence under such circumstances, institutions are likely to be more deeply rooted in tradition and in the habits and human nature of the individuals of which the community is composed. In the natural course institutions may thus come to exist less as instruments for the performance of social functions than as interests of their functionaries or of one of the several classes of which the community is composed. In the latter case they are likely to impose themselves as a discipline and as external forms of control upon the generations that grow up under the influence of their tradition.

Much more might be said in regard to the manner in which social movements initiate and are eventually superseded by institutions. Social movements seem, in many instances, to be the source and origin not merely of new institutions but of new societies. But there are other aspects of collective behavior which, for the purposes of this paper, are more interesting and significant.

Sumner distinguishes between (1) institutions which are enacted and (2) institutions which are crescive—that is, institutions which grow up and take form in the course of the historic process and those which, insofar as they are the products of reflection and rational purpose, have the character of an artifact rather than of an organism. In the long run, however, every institution will tend to have the character of something that is at least indigenous to the situation and the society in which it exists. The distinction Sumner makes is obvious enough. We do set up institutions and expect them to go like machines. Society is always more or less a work of art. On the other hand, institutions are always, finally, the accumulated effects of tradition and custom; they are always in process of becoming what they were predestined to be, human nature being what it is, rather than what they are and were.

There is, as Sumner says, implicit in every institution a concept and a philosophy. In the efforts of men acting together to pursue a consistent course of action in a changing world this concept emerges and the philosophy which was implicit becomes explicit. It may take the form of a rationalization or a justification for the institution's existence—what might be described as the institution's *apologia pro vita sua*. Although there may be implicit in the practices of every institution an idea and a philosophy, it is only in a changing society where it becomes necessary to defend or redefine its functions that this philosophy is likely to achieve a formal and dogmatic statement; and even then the body of sentiment and ideas which support these principles may remain, like an iceberg, more or less completely submerged in the "collective unconscious," whatever that is. It is furthermore only in a political society, in which a public exists that permits discussion, rather than in a society organized on a familial and authoritative basis that rational principles tend to supersede tradition and custom as a basis of organization and control. Besides, mankind has never been as completely rational in either its behavior or its thinking as was once supposed. As Sumner remarks, "property, marriage, and religion are still almost entirely in the mores."[6]

It is, however, in the nature of political society that every class, caste, institution, or other functional unit should have its own dogma and its individual life-program. In a familial society, dogma and ideology may perhaps be said to exist potentially and in the egg. They are not so likely to be stated formally as a rule or principle of action.

One of the recent extensions of the realm of the social has been the inclusion in the field of sociological investigation of the subject of knowledge itself. "The principal thesis of a sociology of knowledge is," as Mannheim has stated it, "that there are modes of thought which cannot be adequately understood as long as their social origins are obscured."[7]

6 William Graham Sumner, *Folkways* (New York: Ginn & Co., 1906), p. 54.

7 Karl Mannheim, *Ideology and Utopia* (New York: Harcourt, Brace & Co., 1936), p. 2.

This means that, from the point of a sociology of collective behavior, the ideology of a society or of a social group is, like its customs and its folkways, an integral part of its social structure and that one can no longer proceed on the assumption that "the single individual thinks. Rather it is more correct to insist that he participates in thinking further what other men have thought before him."[8]

The ideology of a class, caste, or social group seems to perform the same role in the functioning of a collective unit that the individual's conception of himself performs in the function of his personality. As the individual's conception of himself projects his acts into the future and in that fashion serves to control and direct the course of his career, so in the case of a society its ideology may be said to direct, control, and give consistency, in the vicissitudes of a changing world, to its collective acts.

The psychiatrists seem to have been the first to direct attention to the importance of the individual's self-consciousness in the understanding of his behavior. They were, also, among the first to take account of the fact that the individual's conception of himself, as long as he is socially oriented and sane, is always a more or less accurate reflection of his status in one or more social groups.

In somewhat the same fashion sociologists, some of whom got their inspiration and took their point of departure from Karl Marx, have arrived at the conclusion that the ideologies, not merely of economic classes but of cultural groups generally, are a by-product of their collective acts. "It is not," as Mannheim puts it, "men in general who think, or even isolated individuals who do the thinking, but men in certain groups who have developed a particular style of thought in an endless series of responses to certain typical situations characterizing their common position."[9]

This extension of the field of sociological investigation to include the natural history of the ideas, ideologies, intellectual dogmas, and those unconscious understandings which make concert, collective action, and above all conversation and discussion, possible, has brought within the purview of systematic investiga-

8 Ibid., p. 3.
9 Ibid., p. 3.

tion those very elements, in personality and in society, namely, the conceptual and rational, which scholasticism had forever put beyond the sphere of an empirical science and the possibility of a naturalistic explanation.

The theory that the state is a legal construction and in that sense a logical artifact has remained the last stronghold of a sociology that conceives of itself as a philosophy rather than as a natural or empirical science. As a matter of fact the sociology of knowledge might well serve as prolegomena to the study of what has sometimes been referred to, although in the language which Mannheim expressly repudiates, as the "group mind."[10] The rather ghostly conceptions, "group thinking," "group mind," including the "general will," have haunted the minds of writers on political science and sociology, whenever and wherever they have tried to conceive the intrinsic nature of the bond which holds men together in such manner as makes collective action possible.

Almost the first attempt to investigate and describe collective behavior was Gustave Le Bon's volume, *The Crowd: A Study of Popular Mind*.[11] The character of the crowd, or of the psychological crowd, as Le Bon described it, was that of a heterogeneous group which, under the influence of some contagious excitement, had achieved a momentary but relatively complete moral solidarity in which every individual was completely submerged and dominated by the mood and purpose of the group as a whole. He said:

> The psychological crowd is a provisional being formed of heterogeneous elements, which for a moment are combined, exactly as the cells which constitute a living body form by their reunion a new being which displays characteristics very different from these possessed by each of the cells singly.[12]

But the solidarity by which a heterogeneous and casually assembled collection of individuals is transformed into a "new being" is, naturally, not anything physical. It is, to use Le Bon's

10 Ibid., p. 2.

11 New York, 1900; see also Park and Burgess, *Introduction to the Science of Sociology* (Chicago: University of Chicago Press, 1924 ed.), p. 869.

12 Ibid., p. 889.

term, "psychological." The crowd, when organized, behaves according to the "law of the mental unity of crowds," and it is just the consensus and moral solidarity thus achieved which Le Bon describes as the "mind of the crowd," which gives that *omnium-gatherum* the character of a social entity.

In contrast with the organized or psychological crowd is the crowd in dissolution, i.e., the crowd in a state of panic, a stampede. In such a stampede the excitement may be quite as contagious as it is in the organized crowd but it will not express itself in a collective act. On the contrary, the crowd in a state of panic acts as if every individual were for himself and "devil take the hindmost."

Le Bon, more than any other writer, has been able to lend to his conception of the collective mind a sense of reality which is lacking in other descriptions of the same phenomenon. Mary Austin, who writes interestingly but somewhat mystically of the behavior of sheep and shepherds, speaks of the "flock mind." Elsewhere we hear of the "public mind" or the "medieval" or the "modern" mind where, in the context, we are not certain whether those terms refer to an individual type or to a collective unit.

However, none of these is the kind of social unit with which Mannheim is concerned in his studies of the sociology of knowledge. The collective mind which he has sought to investigate is not that of a crowd where there is complete unanimity but rather that of a public where there is diversity of sentiments and of opinion. Nevertheless there is in such a public an underlying and more or less unconscious unanimity of purpose and intent. Consensus, under the circumstances, takes a more complex form which in logic is described as a "universe of discourse." One purpose of Mannheim's studies seems to have been to bring into clear consciousness this underlying unity and identity of intent which exists, or may exist, within the obvious diversity of opinions and attitudes. Characteristic of a public or any group involved in conversation and discussion is what I may describe as the dialectical process. But the dialectical movement of thought, in the course of discussion, tends to assume the character of a collective act.[13]

13 George H. Mead, *Mind, Self, and Society* (Chicago: University of Chicago Press, 1934), p. 7 n.

The group mind, so called, whatever else the implication attached to the term, is always the product of communication. But this communication takes different forms in the crowd and the public. In the case of the mob or the psychological crowd communication takes place, to be sure, but individual A is not able to distinguish his own attitude from that of B, and vice versa. As Mead puts it, "One form does not know that communication is taking place with the other." Le Bon seeks to express the same idea when he describes as one of the incidents of the formation of a crowd the "disappearance of conscious personality and the turning of feeling and thoughts in a definite direction."[14]

In the public, communication takes the form of a conversation; an interchange of attitudes or, as Mead describes it, a "communication of gestures." In this form of communication individual A becomes aware of his own attitude by taking the role of B. In this way A sees his own act from the point of view of B and each participates, from his own point of view, in the collective act. This, says Mead, "carries the process of cooperative activity farther than it can be carried in the herd as such, or in the insect society."[15]

III. *Plant Communities and Animal Societies*

In the meantime there has drawn up on the margins, if not quite within the framework of the social sciences, a body of organized knowledge that calls itself sometimes biological but more often sociological, but is, in any case, concerned with relations that are not ordinarily regarded as social; and it is concerned also with organisms, like plants and animals, which live together in forms of association that do not, in the sense that the term social applies to human beings, constitute them a society. Such, for example, are the plant associations, first observed and described by plant geographers, one of whom was the Danish ecologist, Eugenius Warming.

In 1895 Warming published a volume entitled *Plantesamfund* [Plant Community] in which he described the different plant spe-

14 Park and Burgess, *Introduction*, p. 887.
15 Mead, *Mind, Self, and Society*, pp. 253–55.

cies living together within the limits of a habitat as "practicing" a kind of natural economy and by so doing maintaining relations which constituted them a natural community. It is this economy and this community which is the special subject matter of the science of ecology.[16] Ecology has been described as "an extension of economics to the whole world of life."[17] But it is at the same time, as Charles Elton put it, not so much a new subject as a new name for an old one. It is a kind of natural history.[18]

A vast literature has come into existence since Warming's first attempt to describe and systematize what was known at that time of the communal life of plants, and this literature has been succeeded in turn by similar studies of plant and animal communities as well as of insect and animal societies. Ecology is concerned with communities rather than societies, though it is not easy to distinguish between them. Plant and animal sociology seems to include both forms of association. A plant community is, however, an association of diverse species. An animal society is more likely to be, like insect societies, an association of familial or genetic origin.

The first ecological studies were, however, geographical, concerned quite as much with the migration and distribution of plants and animals as with their dependence upon their physical habitats. More recently, following a cue suggested by Darwin in his *Origin of Species*, ecological studies have investigated not merely the interactions and interdependencies of the plants and of plants and animals, including man, living in the same habitat but they have

16 Ecology is a term first used by Ernest Haeckel, the distinguished German biologist, in 1878, and is derived from the Greek *oikos*, which means house and is the root from which the word economics was coined.

17 H. G. Wells, Julian S. Huxley, and G. P. Wells, *The Science of Life*, vol. 3 (New York: Doubleday, Doran & Co., 1931), chap. 5, p. 961.

18 *Animal Ecology* (New York: Macmillan Co., 1927), p. 1; "Species that form a community must either practice the same economy, making approximately the same demands on its environment [as regards nourishment, light, moisture, etc.], or one species present must be dependent for its existence upon another species, sometimes to such an extent that . . . symbiosis seems to prevail between them" (Eugenius Warming, *Oecology of Plants* [Oxford, 1909], p. 12).

studied the biotic community itself insofar as it seemed to exhibit a unitary or organismic character. This emphasis upon the communal organization of plants and animals has more and more disposed students to describe the social and ecological relations of all living organisms in the language of the social sciences, of economics, of sociology, and even of political science.

Recently, W. C. Allee published a volume[19] which he described as "A Study of General Sociology." It was, in fact, a sort of first book of animal sociology since it dealt with what happens to animals when they come together temporarily in large numbers, like bats in a cave or bees in a swarm. These associations were inevitably, under the circumstances, of the elementary and abstract sort which mere propinquity enforces. Such aggregations are, in fact, mere population units in which there is spatial integration, to be sure, but no indication of social solidarity.

This publication was followed by the translation from the German of an imposing volume by J. Braun-Blanquet,[20] in which the complexities of the interrelations and interactions of the plants and plant species that constitute a plant community—including the physical conditions under which this communal life is maintained—are systematically analyzed and described.

Ecology is, it seems, in the way of becoming a social, without ceasing to be a biological science. It is still concerned with the physical conditions which make plant and animal life possible, but the life for which these conditions exist, is not that of the different species merely but of some sort of social entity or superorganism of which the species are integral parts.

The effect of this extension of the concept of society and the social to include every form of association short of parasitism in which organisms of the same or different species practice a natural economy seems to extend indefinitely the number and the variety of social relationships and of social entities with which a general sociology is concerned. "The whole field of interrelationships of organisms," says Allee, "must be taken as the content of a general

19 *Animal Aggregations* (Chicago: University of Chicago Press, 1931).

20 *Plant Sociology* (New York: McGraw-Hill Book Co., Inc., 1932).

sociology."[21] This conception of the social indicates a wide field for taxonomic explorations since it suggests that the realm of the social is coterminous with the active interaction of living organisms in what Darwin described as "the web of life." It is in this sense that Darwin's theory of the origin of the species may be regarded, as J. Arthur Thomson says, as an application of a sociological principle to the facts of natural history.

Meanwhile the area within which a worldwide struggle for existence is operative is steadily expanding and, seeing that microbes travel by the same means as men, the dangers of disease and the dangers of war tend to grow *pari passu* with increased use of every form of transportation, including the most recent, the airplane. Thus the web of life which holds within its meshes all living organisms is visibly tightening, and there is in every part of the world obviously a growing interdependence of all living creatures; a vital interdependence that is more extensive and intimate today than at any other period in the course of the long historical process.

In spite of the extraordinary variety of associations which the studies of the plant and animal sociologists have revealed, all or most of the more general types seem to be represented in human society. In fact one thing that makes the study of plant and animal associations interesting is that plant and animal communities so frequently exhibit, in strangely different contexts, forms of associations that are fundamentally like those with which we are familiar in human society. Besides, they exhibit, singly and in isolation, types of association which in human society are overlaid by other later and more elaborate forms. For example, the plant community is an association in which the relations between individual species may be described as purely economic. The plant community, in other words, is not, as is the case of insect and animal societies, a genetic association in which the individual units are held together by natural and instinctive ties of family and the necessities of procreation and the protection of the young.

Plants cast down their seeds on the ground from whence they are borne away on wind, wave, or any other convenience which

21 Allee, *Animal Aggregations*, p. 37.

chance offers. Thus plants once established on the soil and in a habitat are obviously immobile, but the plant species are more easily and widely dispersed than animals. Plants of the same species, because they make the same demands upon the natural resources of the habitat, are likely to be dispersed by competition. For the same reason plants which make different demands upon the natural resources—i.e., light, moisture, and the chemical elements which they take from the soil and air—tend to become associated because, as each species finds its niche in the community, competition is diminished and the total production of the plant community, if one may speak of production in this connection, is increased.

Plant communities do not, of course, act collectively as animals do, but the associations they form, partly by a natural selection of species and partly by adaptation and accommodation of individuals—as in the case of the vine and the fig tree—do, by diminishing competition within and by resisting invasion from without, make more secure the life of the community and of the individuals of which it is composed.

The plant community is perhaps the only form of association in which competition is free and unrestricted, and even there competition is limited to some extent by the mere passive resistance offered by the association and coordination of different species of which the community is composed. This limitation of competition is, however, purely external and not the result, as in the case of animals and man, of either instinctive or intelligent inhibition.[22]

The needs of plants as of every other organism are twofold. There is the need to preserve the individual in his struggle to complete his own life cycle and there is the need of preserving the continued existence of the species. Plants provide these two necessities, however, in ways that differ fundamentally from ani-

22 "Primitive man, just as much as civilized man, has his own strong inward and outward ties and inhibitions beyond which he cannot go (Thurnwald); and the behavior of an animal is determined in exactly the same way by the inner and outer restraints which are imposed upon it. Whosoever believes that sexual inhibitions do not exist for animals is on the wrong road altogether" (Friedrich Alverdes, *Social Life in the Animal World* [New York, 1927], pp. 12–13).

mals or at least from those animals that maintain a family and a social existence. Braun-Blanquet says:

> The principles of usefulness, of division of labor, of conscious support, of marshaling all resources for the accomplishment of a common purpose do not exist in the plant world. The struggle for existence rules here undisturbed. It regulates directly or indirectly all the unconscious expressions of the social life of plants. Herein lies the deep and fundamental difference between the vital relations of plant and those of animal communities.[23]

Insect societies, as contrasted with the freedom and anarchy of plant communities, are well-nigh perfect examples of an industrial regimentation and of a communism in which the individual is completely subordinated to the interests of the society. The explanation is that insect societies are merely large families in which the functions, not only of the sexes but of so-called castes, are fixed at birth in their physiological structure.[24]

This does not mean that there is in insect societies nothing that corresponds to the symbiotic forms of association characteristic of plant communities. On the contrary, social insects, notably the social ants, live in symbiotic relation with a number of other insects. In fact, as Wheeler remarks, "ants may be said to have domesti-

23 Braun-Blanquet, *Plant Sociology*, p. 5.

24 "In striking contrast with men, ants have to be built for their jobs. They do not make tools; they grow them as parts of their bodies. . . . Each species of ant is thus built specially for its own particular kind of life and is quite unadaptable to any other. Even within the single community there is the same kind of specialized physical diversity. Only the males and females have wings; the neuters grow up wingless. The neuters have much bigger brains than the males or the queens; but, as they never have to fly, their eyes are smaller. . . . This physical diversity goes hand in hand with diversity of behaviour. The males do nothing but fertilize the queens when the time comes. The queens lay eggs eternally. The workers have the instinct of tending the young, the soldiers are impelled to bite and snap in defence of the colony. The workers of one kind of ant keep ant-cows, but never look at grain or make raids on other ants. Those of a second are only graminivorous, those of a third live by slave-labour. Thus the division of labour in an ant-community, unlike the division of labour in a human community, is based on marked, inborn individual differences of structure and instinctive behaviour between its members" (Wells, Huxley, and Wells, *Science of Life*, 4:1163–64).

cated a greater number of animals than we have and the same statement may prove to be true of their food plants which have been carefully studied."[25]

It is more difficult in the case of the social animals than of the social insects to define the difference between forms of association that are symbiotic and those which are social. Thus Alverdes[26] distinguishes between what he calls associations (mere collections) and societies. By associations he means those aggregations of animals that otherwise carry on a solitary existence, but do, at some period in their seasonal or life cycle, come together in response to occasional and external causes. By societies, on the other hand, he means those more permanent groups, including insect societies, in which individuals come together in response to the needs and instinctive urges of the individual organisms. This means that the form which an animal society does take is the one it was predestined to assume by the nature of the inheritance of the individuals of which it was composed. "In short," says Alverdes, "no social instinct, no society."

There are two types of association, aside from those occasional aggregations already referred to, which may have arisen in response to "instincts" rather than to external forces. These are the family and the herd or flock. In both cases the particular form which solidarity takes undoubtedly has an inherited and instinctive basis. What operates to modify this form of association and determine the collective activities of the individuals so associated is, among other things, the character of the communication of which the group is capable. Thus among the anthropoid apes, as among the birds, there seems to exist, as there frequently does between a man and his dog, a responsiveness, an understanding and intimacy not unlike that characteristic of personal relations among human beings.[27]

25 Wheeler, *Social Life among Insects*, p. 17.

26 Alverdes, *Social Life in the Animal World*, pp. 14–16.

27 Wolfgang Köhler, *The Mentality of Apes* (New York: Harcourt, Brace & Co., Inc., 1927), appendix, "Some Contributions to the Psychology of Chimpanzees," particularly pp. 282–311; see also Alverdes, *Social Life in the Animal World*, "Mutual Understanding and Imitation," chap. 9, pp. 164–78.

The extent to which animals of the herd or flock are responsive to the expressive behavior of other animals is most obvious on the occasions where some excitement, whipped up by the milling of the herd or flock, mounts to a point where it issues in a panic or stampede. The milling herd is in so many respects like the organized crowd, as Le Bon has conceived it, that one wonders that it does not, as in the case of a mob, express its excitement in a collective act. The mob is, in fact, the crowd that acts. But a stampede, because in this case the impulses and actions of the individuals involved are not so coordinated, does not take the form of a collective act. There is no stampede "mind."

The herd does not act but it does, in the course of its milling about, perform something that might be called a dance. Mary Austin says:

> It is doubtful if the herder is anything more to the flock than an incident of the range, except as a giver of salt, for the only cry they make to him is the salt cry. When the natural craving is at the point of urgency they circle about his camp or his cabin, leaving off feeding for that business; and nothing else offering, they will continue this headlong circling about a boulder or any object bulking large in their immediate neighborhood remotely resembling the appurtenances of man, as if they had learned nothing since they were free to find licks for themselves, except that salt comes by bestowal and in conjunction with the vaguely indeterminant lumps of matter that associate with man. . . . This one quavering bleat, (the salt cry), unmistakable to the sheepman even at a distance, is the only new note in the sheep's vocabulary, and the only one which passes with intention from himself to man. As for the call of distress which a leader raised by hand may make to his master, it is not new, is not common to flock usage, and is swamped utterly in the obsession of the flock-mind.[28]

Why does this dance of the restless flock not, as Mary Austin's description suggests it might, assume the form of a ceremony? Why, in other words, does this collective excitement not take on the character of ritual or a symbolic act? The mass games described by Groos (*The Play of Animals*) and the sham, and sometimes very real, battles in which birds and other animals engage during

28 *The Flock* (Boston: Houghton Mifflin & Co., 1906), pp. 127–29.

the mating season, seem to be fundamentally expressive, merely. Groos calls them orgiastic in character.[29]

Mass behavior of that sort in animals is not unlike the same expressive and orgiastic behavior in human beings, since the crowd that dances rather than acts is at any rate a "psychological" if not an "organized" crowd. The behavior of animals under the influence of collective excitement is to such an extent like that of crowds everywhere that Alverdes, in his effort to indicate the character of the solidarity which is created by the rise in the herd of this contagious excitement, has recourse again to the conception of the "collective mind." This phrase cannot, however, be regarded as an explanation of the phenomena to which it refers. It may be, like the "instincts" to which Alverdes refers in his description of animal society, inexplicable. In that case "collective mind" is merely the name we give to a phenomenon that needs to be further investigated.

What are these phenomena? Alverdes says:

> Among the social species, courage and pugnacity grow in proportion to the number of individuals present; this is true of ants, bees, bumble bees, wasps, hornets, and others. In the case of the honey bee, a small and weak community often does not defend itself against enemies which it could easily repulse, whereas a strong community is always ready for attack, and expels every intruder. According to Forel, one and the same ant which is full of courage among its fellows will take to flight before a much weaker adversary as soon as it finds itself alone. State-building insects are overcome by profound depression if their nest disappears.[30]

What distinguishes the collective mind of the lower animals from that of the human crowd is the fact that the contagious excitements which arise in the herd do not, as in the case of the psychological crowd, issue in either collective action or in anything like ceremonial behavior. What is even more significant, these excitements do not finally take the form of institutions. It is the possession of institutions which distinguishes human from animal

29 Alverdes, *Social Life in the Animal World*, pp. 144–51.
30 Ibid., p. 142.

societies. Institutions, however, seem to be, finally, the product of the type of dialectical or rational communication which is the peculiar characteristic of human beings.

IV. *Socialization*

This brief survey of the forms of association, the communal and social, in which individual organisms maintain some sort of collective existence, suggests that it is pertinent to repeat here in regard to socialization—the process by which associations are formed—what was said earlier, in somewhat different language, in regard to two types of association, or two aspects of society. Socialization and social organization seem at any rate to be brought about by the cooperation of two fundamental types of interaction. There is in every society a process or processes of individuation and a process or processes of integration. The effect of competition is to disperse existing aggregations of organisms and by so doing to bring about, as a result of adaptation to new environments, the creation of new races and species. But the existence within a habitat of diverse species and races makes possible a new association and a natural economy, based on genetic diversity rather than genetic identity.

In human societies a divison of labor based upon a diversity of occupations and enforced by economic competition performs the function which, in the plant community or other biotic associations, is performed by symbiosis.

There is, however, or there presently emerges in both animal and human societies, the necessity for a more stable form of association than that which either biotic or economic competition and cooperation is sufficient to produce. Such a more stable form of association is likely to occur whenever the interaction of the competing organisms, by adaptation to the habitat or in any other fashion, achieves a relatively stable equilibrium. In such a situation, with the gradual rise in the animal species of a capacity for and means of communication—by which animals as well as human beings have been able to respond to the minds and intentions of other animals—a new and more intimate type of solidarity is made possible; a solidarity which enables societies to coordinate and direct the acts of their individual components in accordance with the interests and purposes of the society as a whole.

Thus a society may be said to arise upon the basis of a community. The distinction is that in the community, as in the case of the plant and animal community, the nexus which unites individuals of which the community is composed is some kind of symbiosis or some form of division of labor. A society, on the other hand, is constituted by a more intimate form of association based on communication, consensus, and custom.

The social organism, as Herbert Spencer conceived it, was based on the existence in society of a division of labor. It is in this sense, also, that F. E. Clements and others have described the plant community as an organism.[31] But the social organism thus conceived had, as Spencer points out, no sensorium. There was no central apparatus where the sensations and impulses of the individual units of which a society is composed could be sorted out, assimilated, and integrated, so that society could act consistently in response to them. Society and the superorganism have, to be sure, no sensorium, but individuals in society do communicate and somehow they do achieve that sort of consensus that Comte believed was the essential and fundamental trait of any society. This communication and the accumulated body of tradition on which it is based is what is sometimes referred to as the "collective mind."

Society, theoretically at least, begins as Allee pointed out, with a mere aggregation, i.e., a population unit. But even on this level of association there is interaction of some sort. On the economic level, as we know economic relations in human society, competition and the struggle for existence continue, but as social relations multiply this struggle is more and more restricted by understandings, by customs, by formal and contractual relations, and by law. All of these impose restrictions, in the interest of an evolving society and of the manifold social and collective units of

31 Braun-Blanquet, *Plant Sociology*, p. 21.

which such a society is composed, upon the free competition of individuals in the original aggregate or population unit.

On the political level the freedom and competition of individuals is still further limited by the express recognition of the superior and sovereign interests and rights of the state or of the community as a whole, as against the adverse interests or claims of individuals or groups of individuals, living within or under the protection of the state or other political authority. The existence of such sovereignty as the state exercises, however, is dependent upon the existence of a solidarity within the state or other territorial and political unit, sufficient to maintain that authority and enforce its behests when they come into conflict with the interests and the purposes of individuals.

Eventually this competition of individuals is restricted and restrained on the personal and moral level of association by the claims which intimate associations with, and knowledge of, the needs, the attitudes, and the sentiments of others make upon us, particularly when these are reinforced by tradition, customs, and the normal expectations of mankind. Every individual who is or will eventually be incorporated into any society, whether it be an alien coming from some other ethnic or cultural group or one born into the association and society of which he is a member, inevitably passes through such a process of socialization. The process of socialization as it takes place in the formation of any social group today reflects in a way the phylogenic processes by which existing types of association, or societies, and of institutions have come into existence in the course of the historic process.

Looked at in a historical perspective we observe that the progressive socialization of the world, that is, the incorporation of all the peoples of the earth in a worldwide economy, which has laid the foundation for the rising worldwide political and moral order —the great society—is but a repetition of the processes that take place wherever and whenever individuals come together to carry on a common life and to form the institutions—economic, political, or cultural—to make that common life effective.

But below the level of those forms of associations which we

call social is the biotic community and the ecological organization in which man finds himself involved in competition and cooperation with all other living organisms. Thus we may represent human society as a kind of cone or triangle, of which the basis is the ecological organization of human beings living together in a territorial unit, region, or natural area. On this level the struggle for existence may go on, will go on, unobserved and relatively unrestricted.

If one is an alien he may live in the new society for a considerable time in a relationship which is essentially symbiotic, that is, a relationship in which he does not feel the pressure of the customs and expectations of the society by which he is surrounded. Or he may, if he is conscious of the social pressure, still experience it as something alien to him and continue to treat the people with whom he comes in contact as part of the flora and fauna, a situation in which their social pressures would impose upon him no moral claims which he felt bound to respect. But eventually the mere presence of an alien who is possessed by such a dispassionate and secular attitude toward the customs, conventions, and ideals of the society of which he has become, by the effect of propinquity and whether he chose to be or not, a constituent element, is certain to bring him, no matter how discrete his behavior, into conflict with those to whom their customs, if not sacred, are at least to such an extent accepted; that a too great detachment toward them is certain to be offensive if not a little shocking. Such an alien attitude, in any case, inevitably stimulates in the native a pervasive sense of malaise as if in the presence of something not quite understood and hence always a little to be feared.

This is not, of course, the only way so-called "culture conflicts" may arise. It is, perhaps, the most insidious form in which they are likely to appear. Conflict, which is merely conscious competition—that is, competition in a situation in which the competitor knows with whom and with what he is competing—creates, to be sure, a solidarity in the competing groups. Solidarity in the in-group, as Sumner has pointed out, is always more or less an effect of conflict with an out-group.

Conflict is, however, like competition, an individuating factor in society. It affects the individual not merely in his vocation and in his position in the economic order but affects him in his personal relations. It affects his status and very largely determines the conception which he forms of himself. It is in conflict situations that economic competition, the struggle for a livelihood, tends to become a struggle for political and social status.

However, conflict leads to understandings; understandings not merely implicit but explicit and formal. Conflict is the most elementary form of political behavior, and formal understandings, involving controversy and discussion, terminate in accommodations, in the formation of classes, and in formal and contractual relations of various sorts. Political conflict, when it does not lead to the formation of classes, does at least bring about class consciousness, and politics seem to be merely the classic and typical form in which the class struggle is carried on.

More intimate associations in the family and in the neighborhood as well as by occupation and class tend to develop more intimate personal understandings. Particularly is this the case within the limits of what Cooley calls the "primary group," i.e., the family, the neighborhood, and the village.

The process of socialization may be said to terminate in assimilation, which involves the more or less complete incorporation of the individual into the existing moral order as well as the more or less complete inhibition of competition. Under these circumstances conflict takes the form of rivalry, more or less generous.

The child born into a society may be said to go through the same process of socialization as the stranger who is finally adopted into a new society. The difference is that in the child's case the process begins with assimilation and ends with individuation and emancipation, i.e., emancipation from the traditions and claims of the family and primary group. The process of individuation ordinarily continues with his participation in an ever wider circle of political and economic association. The child's life begins, to be sure, without those human traits that we describe as personal. Most of the child's personality traits seem to be acquired in intimate associations with other human beings. But children are very rapidly and very completely incorporated into the societies in which birth or chance finds them. Only gradually do they achieve the independence and individuality we associate with maturity. One is assimilated into the little world of the family, but he achieves independence and individuality in the larger, freer world of men and affairs.

One begins life as an individual organism involved in a struggle with other organisms for mere existence. It is this elementary form of association that we describe as ecological. One becomes involved later in personal and moral, eventually economic and occupational, and ultimately political, associations; in short, with all the forms of association we call social. In this way society and the person, or, the socialized individual, came into existence as a result of essentially the same social processes and as a result of the same cycle or succession of events.

Index